RUST BELT ARCANA
TAROT AND NATURAL HISTORY IN THE EXURBAN WILDS

RUST BELT ARCANA

TAROT AND NATURAL HISTORY IN THE EXURBAN WILDS

Matt Stansberry
with illustrations by David Wilson

Belt Publishing

First edition 2018

ISBN: 978-1-948742-12-2

Belt Publishing
1667 E 40th Street
Suite #1G1
Cleveland OH 44103

Book design by Meredith Pangrace & David Wilson
Cover by David Wilson

TABLE OF CONTENTS

INTRODUCTION

Good prophecy is always given in riddles, for the gods do not reveal their every secret… They only open a way and wait for mortal nobility or depravity to take its natural course.

—Loren Eiseley

One bleary morning on a layover at O'Hare airport in Chicago, I was flipping through checklists of animal and plant species published by the Cleveland Metroparks. Each folding pamphlet listed dozens of species most of us have never seen, or even considered—animals and plants living secret lives alongside us on the southern shore of Lake Erie. And my mind inexplicably leapt to the Tarot.

Something sparked. I wondered: could the images and ideas represented in tarot cards match up to scenarios in the natural world? I spent the next two years diving into the world of the arcana (mysteries) of Tarot, and it's been a witchy, spiritual trip.

People have used tarot cards for over 500 years to reveal hidden information about their lives, their psyches, and their futures. Some people believe tarot cards to be a map of Jung's collective subconscious. Others suggest the Tarot conveys occult, esoteric knowledge. Each user projects their own experiences, beliefs, fears, and desires onto the cards.

In a traditional tarot deck there are seventy-eight cards —fifty-six cards resembling a standard playing card deck, and twenty-two special cards that are outside of the numbered and suited sequence.

These twenty-two cards are known as the Major Arcana, and each of them has accrued a set of meanings or associations over time.

The essays in this book map those divinatory associations and signifiers in the cards to the wildlife of the Rust Belt. These are stories of abundance and loss, the persistent remnant wilderness of the industrial Midwest. Exploring this natural history helps us to find our place in the landscape, to know our home and ourselves.

For example:

The Fool: A young bear is cast off from its mother in the spring to wander a fragmented suburban forest, to raid bird feeders, to be harried by dogs and traffic, chased through golf courses and farms.

The Magician: An ocean-going trout from the Pacific Ocean climbs industrial, sewage-tainted rivers in the Midwest. The river is both sick and healthy, the trout is both wild and made.

The High Priestess: The snowy owl seems vulnerable and lost by day, hunts by moonlight on the frozen lakes for seabirds. How will a rapidly warming Arctic affect this raptor's survival?

The Empress: A thousand-year-old plant defies winter by warming its core to seventy-two degrees Fahrenheit, melting through snow and ice to emit a scent that mimics a rotting corpse.

Early on in the writing process, I remember meditating under an old white oak tree. I was reading books on shamanism. I felt like I understood Carlos Casteneda. I was buying crystals.

At other points, I was slogging through every Great Lakes-area biologist's master thesis in my library.

I begged my network of naturalist friends to find me somebody—anybody—with something interesting to say about a goddamn opossum.

Ultimately, this is a book about how mindful interactions with common animals can enrich our lives and our understanding of ourselves. It is about looking at bugs and fish and birds with devotion. It is about participating in their world.

0

THE FOOL

CHAPTER 0
THE FOOL'S JOURNEY

It had been in the spring of his second year when his mother ran him off, snapping at his flanks.

The young bear turned in disbelief as his protector and companion pushed him to leave. Where would he go? Away from his mother's territory before a larger roving male found him lurking.

He slunk away distraught and hungry, always hungry. The bear in spring ate constantly. He found squawroot and skunk cabbage, stripped catkins off trees. It was a lean time for the young bear.

He ambled west, adrift in the world without a family, a territory—without an identity. The bear walked alone into an unknowable future.

Pennsylvania's black bear population had experienced a fivefold increase since the 1970s, to 20,000 animals.

A male bear might roam 200 square miles in a single year, whereas female bears defend fixed territories, maintain complex family hierarchies, and carve out a niche in their mother's range.

Increasingly, young male bears cast out of their mother's territories in the wilds of Western Pennsylvania wander over the border into Ohio. Biologists estimate between 50 and 100 animals have recolonized the eastern corner of the state.

A young Pennsylvanian bear had roamed through miles of fragmented, deer-bitten forest. It crossed dozens of roads, raided backyard birdfeeders, and scrambled through highly populated areas until it had settled in a suburban park northeast of Akron.

For a year the bear lived in a patch of woods stranded between a golf course, baseball fields, and tens of thousands of homes, hibernating in a hidden den somewhere throughout the winter.

No one had seen the bear recently—it had moved on. But the local park district commemorated the event by installing a life-sized resin sculpture of a black bear, complete with paw prints and epoxy bear scat at the nature center.

I came to these woods to see what had held the wandering bear's interest, to try to walk in its footsteps, to see this place as the bear had seen it.

The floor of the beech-maple forest was messy in the early fall, covered in fallen tree trunks and grape tangles. I dropped to my knees near a rotten log and rended it with clawed hands, like a bear. The wet pulp spilled out between my fingers and I looked for what nutrition might be hiding: some slugs, millipedes, spiders —mostly chitin.

I perked up my ears, listening to the relentless susurration of tires on a nearby highway and the chitter of downy woodpeckers. Confident that hikers wouldn't come upon me unaware while I crawled in the dirt, I moved to a new log and turned it over, tore open the bark, sought out what might be edible, hiding inside.

It's not hard to imagine that we and bears share a similar sense of mind.

In 2012, a prominent group of neuroscientists declared that non-human animals have the capacity to experience emotions, intention, and sense of self.

Animals experience consciousness.

Anyone who has spent time around animals might find this proclamation silly. But science and industry have been loath to assign consciousness to non-human creatures, as so much development, food production, and environmental degradation is conducted under the rationalization that animals are resources, not individuals with volition and memory.

Bears are not insensate automatons, but rather empathetic, expressive animals that express creativity and intelligence.

According to black bear researcher Ben Kilham, bears recognize their reflection in a mirror – they have a sense of identity. Bears project and plan for future events and remember and learn from the past—a concept called recursive thinking. Bears exhibit reciprocity, altruism, and even pantomime—which implies they are not only self-aware, but perceive awareness in others.

In his book *Out on a Limb*, Kilham theorizes that bears developed this cognitive ability and emotional intelligence for the same reason anthropologists suspect humans developed our powerful brains. In a landscape with unevenly distributed resources, individuals and groups will need to negotiate and cooperate in order to survive.

The bear is deeply rooted in the human psyche, and it has shaped our language, how we think.

To bear means to carry or support a weight, to withstand. To bear means to give birth or produce growth.

Bears eat what we eat—whatever is ripe, plentiful, easy to find or kill. We share an openness to opportunity.

"It is the bear's broad, searching, persistent openness that makes contact with us, that flash of recognition in which men instantly perceive a fellow being whose questing provocation, whose garrulous, taciturn, lazy ways, even whose obligations and commitments to the hunt, to hole up, and to dominate the space he lives in are familiar" write Paul Shephard and Barry Sanders in *The Sacred Paw*, a study of the bear's role and symbolism in the human consciousness.

The bear demonstrates free will—a sort of individualist decision making. When you look at a bear you can almost see it weighing its options, considering a wide range of possible alternatives each with its own consequences.

We live parallel lives. We have been constant companions, observing each other from a distance our entire existence as species. We recognize some shared version of consciousness.

Black bears have roamed eastern North America for over a half a million years. In some places they thrive near human populations. But here in this southern corner of the Rust Belt, where the contiguous forests and swamps had been flattened, lit, and paved, there just doesn't seem to be enough room for both bears and us.

After winding through the woods for a half mile, I came upon seventy-five-foot-high sandstone slabs rising out of the forest floor. The rocks slumped together to form a cave.

I crawled inside the opening and looked at the sunlight filtering down through openings in the rocks above. I could see beech tree limbs waving in the breeze. I sat with my notebook and tried to imagine what a young bear might have thought of this place.

This patch of Northeast Ohio, scrawled over by a wandering Cuyahoga River watershed, is largely wooded. There are tens of thousands of acres of public land in various states of protection, succession, and regeneration between the park systems.

The land seems to be recovering. Yet there are more than 4.5 million people living in the surrounding areas.

A group of retirees with small dogs had approached and lingered at the mouth of the cave, and the sound of their conversation echoed through the chamber, setting my teeth on edge. I imagined a poor bear trying to find peace in this place.

How are we to welcome the bear's presence in a world built for human convenience? Where does the bear fit into a society committed to minimizing risk and cost?

This is the borderland—a place where the natural and post-industrial worlds collide and overlap.

In the Tarot tradition, the Fool is an innocent wandering through the world, a traveler represented by the number zero, without attachments, a being of continuous movement and physical needs.

We identify with the Fool. He is the best and the worst of us.

In the popular Rider-Waite tarot deck, the Fool blithely walks through a dangerous world, enraptured with his own gait. He is richly dressed in a floral print and unconcerned that he is about to pitch off a cliff. This iconic image, drawn by illustrator Pamela Colman Smith over a hundred years ago, suggests aspects of the Fool's arrogance, vanity, and naïveté.

This wandering black bear forces us to confront the conflicted nature of this place. The bear in Akron is a miracle and a nuisance. It is a glimpse of the wholeness and truly wild landscape we might hope for, as environmental advocates in a degraded region.

It represents optimism and possibility, and yet also folly. There is no place here for a young bear, let alone one of the 800-pound forest gods stalking the deep woods in the state next door.

It is foolish to want something you can't have, to try something you cannot achieve.

The naive bear gorging on trash cans and suet feeders will be punished. He will be harried by dogs and traffic, chased through golf courses and farms. He will wander without a home, but will endure by instinct.

Cheering for the young bear to ramble over the Ohio landscape is foolish, but it is also crucial to understanding the nature of our home.

The wanderer is a truth teller. We want to welcome the Fool, but we cannot sustain him.

I

THE MAGICIAN

CHAPTER 1
CONJURING STEEL

The river is a trickster.

The Cuyahoga flows south from its headwaters in the farm country thirty miles east of Cleveland, and then turns back on itself to scrawl a U-shaped path back toward Lake Erie. It is the most polluted, but also the most biologically productive watershed in the region. It is sick and wounded, but still full of life.

Massive industrial ships navigate the lower stretch of the river, yet a few miles upstream you could wade across the whole mainstem. Locals call it the Crooked River, as it meanders aimlessly across its floodplain. The Cuyahoga didn't carve this valley by its own force, but rather flows lazily over an ancient, larger river's path.

The river caught fire maybe a dozen times, yet the apocryphal story about its demise is full of half-truths. Its degradation became a symbol and a rallying cry to save other places.

As a son of Akron, I see the Cuyahoga as my home river. We drink from of the headwaters, and flush our shit downstream. Despite decades of running away, I find myself rooted and raising a family on its banks.

It is not a beautiful river—it runs muddy, smells rotten, and its buffer of wildness is a thin veneer. You are not supposed to touch the water, for fear of bacterial infection.

I stand in the Cuyahoga up to my waist, letting the current pull me downriver.

In my pouch, I carry sacred talismans—hand-made effigies of thread, feathers, beads, brightly dyed furs, and holographic

17

tinsels. There is a steel barbed hook in the heart of each offering.

I hold a ten-foot graphite wand in my right hand, and I begin a motion overhead, creating lemniscate loops, expertly casting lines and offerings over the riffled surface of the water.

To the uninitiated, my actions seem strange and arbitrary. But every choice, every movement, is based on years of practice, instinct, and ritual.

I am looking for a connection, an acknowledgement or response from nature. I am imposing meaning and causality on a random world. I am deciphering the hidden relationships between rainfall, the current's swirl over a boulder, the amount of sediment in the water, and the likely behaviors of animals unseen.

I've been a fly fisherman almost my entire life, which is to say a liar. The lie is an act of creation. A deception creates an opening, a crack between worlds—prying a space between what is perceived and accepted, and what might be imagined and possible.

In the tarot tradition, the Magician blurs the line between hero and con man. Every serious angler I know falls somewhere on that continuum.

"The most popular images today of this card show him as serene, powerful, with an infinity sign over his head and pointing his magic wand up towards the heavens as if to draw down divine energy," writes Rachel Pollack in *Tarot Wisdom*. But this noble depiction evolved from an original image of a tabletop grifter with shells and a ball. "The grand Magus of the modern tradition is revealed to have his roots in someone who is at best a street entertainer, and at worst a con artist."

In Norse tradition, Loki invented the first fish nets. In Native American traditions of the Pacific Northwest, Raven created the first fish hooks.

According to Lewis Hyde, author of *Trickster Makes This World*, the mythology of the trickster is the story of intelligence rising from hunger, predators outwitting prey.

"If the brain has cunning, it has it as a consequence of appetite; the blood that lights the mind gets its sugars from the gut," writes Hyde.

I wouldn't eat anything that came out of this river, but the skill and awareness are based on a predatory instinct.

Steelhead swim upstream, trout as thick as my leg. They have dark green spotted backs and pink stripes down their flanks and cheeks. The fresh ones are silver. A large fish might be thirty inches long.

They do not belong here in this brown industrialized watershed, but rather the cold, clean rivers on the other side of the continent.

Steelhead are a sea-run strain of rainbow trout, native to the rivers of the West Coast. Wildlife agencies across the Upper Midwest stock steelhead in Great Lakes tributaries to create a recreational fishery, to give us vestigial hunter-gatherers something to do with our weekends.

Fisheries managers release two million juvenile steelhead in the rivers on the southern shoreline of Lake Erie each spring. The young fish disperse into our freshwater sea, mirroring their life cycle on the Pacific Ocean.

Lake Erie has more urban area, more heavy industry, higher population densities and more agriculture than any other Great Lake. Yet, the biomass of Lake Erie vibrates with a frenetic energy. Lake Erie contains just 2 percent of the water for the entire Great Lakes system, and 50 percent of the fish—more than the other four lakes combined.

Young steelhead gorge on insects and baitfish in the open water. Anywhere from two to six years later, the fish return to the rivers where they were released, to try to spawn.

The state doesn't stock the Cuyahoga. But to paraphrase the great steelhead elegist David James Duncan, when you fail to poison a creek quite to death, you can get visitors from distant realms.

The steelhead that swim up the Cuyahoga do so by choice. Or they are born to this water, as I was.

You can see them in the spring, ragged animals near the end of their lives, paired up on the shallow gravel bars trying to spawn before they die or fall back to the lake.

The warm, silted Cuyahoga with its urban runoff and overflowing municipal sewage is not an ideal habitat for young salmonid eggs. But the feeder streams run cold and clear, and in some years the fish make it.

The Ohio EPA had documented natural reproduction of steelhead in seven tributaries of the Cuyahoga River.

The role of the Magician is to conjure something from nothing, to create meaning from happenstance. The winter is cold and terrible. The river smells like burnt plastic. There are not supposed to be any steelhead in this river. And so I stand in contradiction of all reason, waving my arms over the water.

On a bend in the river, the current quickens over a gravel bar. It spills over stones and broken cinder blocks, and flows into a deep pool against an eroded bank. Trees have fallen and drowned in the deep water creating a matrix of limbs, eddies, and shadows. It is a place to rest after climbing a rapid, to ambush baitfish, to flee predators.

I stand on the shallow side of the bend and cast across the river, skirting the deep pool and the tree limbs with a swimming offering—something pink and vulnerable, an undulating creature the size of my pinky finger, designed to entice or enrage any creature that sees it.

But there is too much current—the fly is ripping past the deepest part of the pool too quickly. I step into the gravel bar, cast again. The river sweeps the fly along and it hangs below the best part of the run. I continue to wade further into the current, to get a more parallel angle on the pool.

The river flows over my knees, pushing my body downstream. I can feel the sand and rocks slipping out from under my feet with each step, swept away in the current. If I fall, the water will fill my waders and my heavy boots, it will sweep me into the trees, and I might drown.

But the angle is perfect now, as I flip the fly into the pool, it swims and dangles in slow motion. The fish is right where it should be, and it grabs the hook and turns. The fish instantly feels the barb, and knows its mistake. It dives for the fast current, using the slab of its heavy body to pull against the line and it stretches and moves away.

As I pull it closer to me, it jumps clear of the water. It is an improbably large animal, tethered to me by a piece of string. The fish exhausts itself, fighting my arms and the current. I use the long rod to glide it onto the bank.

It is a massive animal. When I wrap my hand around the base of its tail, my fingers can't touch. Its muscles hulk and spill over my palm when I hold its body out of the water. Its eyes roll, gills flare, and I let it down into the water again. I unpin the hook from the corner of its mouth, and let it nose back into the current.

For a moment it rests, then it is gone. One snap of that huge tail and it's out of my hand.

It is as if it were never there.

II

THE HIGH PRIESTESS

CHAPTER 2
ARCTIC VISITORS, DARK NIGHTS OF THE SOUL

We find the sleepy white lump flecked with black brush strokes sitting on a grassy margin along a municipal airport runway.

I press against the airport security fence, the binoculars come into focus, and North America's heaviest owl opens its piercing yellow eyes.

You can sense its disapproval, its power held in check. Put-upon and bored by our antics, the owl yawns wide.

Snowy owls arrive on the shore of Lake Erie throughout the winter, unannounced on their own unintelligible schedules. They haunt corn fields, roadside telephone poles, marinas, and parks. But they love airports. Some say the flat expanses of the tarmacs remind the raptors of their natal summer homes on the tundra.

Even in this altered landscape, they still come. Birds from the wildest reaches of the planet land in the heart of industrial cities.

Whenever an owl is found, the birding message boards light up with activity and people travel for hours to see these animals.

Their presence is counterintuitive. The owls do not flee hardship in the Arctic, but rather too much success.

Every few years, lemmings flood various parts of the Arctic tundra with rodents.

Lichens grow slowly, rodent populations grow quickly. The lemmings eat all their resources in a certain area and the population crashes. When food resources grow back, the lemmings explode in a boom cycle of extravagant prey abundance. Adult snowy owls converge on these population explosions, and raise double or triple the usual number of baby owls through the summer.

Owls are territorial, nomadic, demanding—seemingly dignified.

Imagine you are one of a huge cohort of yearling birds, stuffed into a bowl in the dirt wing-to-wing. Your nest mates drive each other nuts the way siblings do. Your doting parents push a never-ending supply of dead rodents down your gullet, they're stacked up outside the nest by the dozen.

You can't imagine ever eating another lemming. As soon as you can escape, you disperse across the northern hemisphere.

The technical term for the population boom is an irruption. In big years, the owls can travel as far south as Florida. Large numbers of owls congregate around the Great Lakes.

Snowy owls tend to rest on the ground and can seem unafraid of humans. Some people mistake apathy for illness or starvation, and try to bring the owls offerings of live pet store mice. As is so often the case, the meddling causes problems—rodent-borne pathogens, habituation to human activity.

The fluffy owl sitting on the matted grass of the half-abandoned Cleveland municipal airport seems vulnerable. But the huntress is in repose. It doesn't need us to feed.

Snowy owls hunt the frozen lake, preying on ducks, grebes, and other seabirds clinging to patches of open water. They are agile fliers, and could pluck a kestrel or snow bunting right out of the sky.

In many ways, the snowy owl in Cleveland embodies the qualities of the High Priestess.

It traveled here not on learned behavior or innate migration instinct, but on its own intuition.

Ornithologists are trapping snowy owls and strapping transmitters to their backs to better understand their travels and behaviors. But we cannot follow beyond the Canadian cell phone system, into the highest arctic regions. Its life is unknowable.

It appears calm, restive—yet by night it stalks the ice floes on the lake.

All of these qualities echo the traditional themes of the High Priestess: intuition, mystery, calmness, water, darkness, and power held in abeyance.

The owl's arrival coincides with the winter solstice. There is a duality at play in the High Priestess and this time of year. We struggle against the darkness, but if we embrace it, the darkness also promises permanence and renewal.

Here on the shore of Lake Erie there are a mere nine hours of pale sun on the solstice.

We cling to the artificial lights of our screens as if they were life rafts in the dark tide, and lamps fill every corner of our homes with electric glare. With the power on, we can create a facsimile of summer, perpetual daytime, productivity, entertainment, and arousal.

But we know it is there at our backs, inexorably closing in—darkness, death, winter, infinitum.

We fight the dark, like children refusing to go to bed. Yet, it is a battle we cannot win.

"If you think of night in the true, philosophical proportion, you must realize that it is the prevailing, the absolute thing," writes Donald Culross Peattie in *An Almanac for Moderns*. "Light, day, burning suns and stars—all are the exception. They are but gleaming jewels spattered on the black cloth of darkness. Throughout the universe and eternity it is night that prevails. It is mother of cosmos, capacious womb of light."

While we perceive darkness, we don't experience it in the same way as the generations before us. Over 99 percent of the population of the U.S. and Europe no longer see the Milky Way, but instead look up to a luminous orange fog of our own creation hanging overhead.

We are sleep deprived, strangled by anxiety, overstimulated. We think and breathe in shallow flitting gasps. We are living in dark times, without true dark.

In *Waking up to the Dark*, author Clark Strand suggests that prior to the Industrial Revolution, humans found oneness with the divine during a wakeful period in the dark. "Darkness has always been invaluable for our health and the health of the natural world, and every living creature suffers from its loss," Strand writes.

Darkness is where myth and spiritual wisdom are born, in this ancient liminal space.

Imagine looking up and seeing the face of eternity every night, to be reminded of our place in the universe by galactic dust winding toward infinity. How would it impact our humility and reverence if we had that perspective?

> *And when you speak to me like this,*
> *I try to remember that the wood and cement walls*
> *Of this room are being swept away now,*
> *Molecule by molecule, in a slow and steady wind,*
> *And nothing at all separates our bodies*
> *From the vast emptiness expanding, and I know*
> *We are sitting in our chairs*
> *Discoursing in the middle of the blackness of space.*

—Pattiann Rogers, "Achieving Perspective"

The snowy owl's world is unwinding.

The surface air temperature in the Arctic for 2016 was the highest in over 100 years. Spring snow cover was the lowest on satellite record, which started in 1967. Arctic temperatures have increased at twice the rate of global average.

The availability of lemmings affects the survival of snowy owls, and cycles of lemming abundance are becoming irregular in some parts of the snowy owl's range. This breakdown in lemming cycles is potentially related to climate-induced changes in the quality and amount of snow. Precipitation patterns are predicted to continue changing as a result of anthropogenic climate change.

The total population of this species is not well monitored in its remote habitat. However, results from the Christmas Bird Count suggest a large decrease in population since about 1970.

Scientist cannot say whether snowy owls are adversely affected by climate-induced changes in the abundance of small mammals. When it can be stated, it will be too late.

It's hard to imagine global warming as the north wind crashes across the lake and into the city.

Beyond the airport runway where the owl sits, five-foot swells are pounding the harbor seawall and the spray is freezing to the walkways, the trees, and rocks. Everything on the lake has a thick rime of ice. The traffic on I-90 behind me is somehow even louder than the wind. The combined sound is like something senseless devouring the world.

How does the snowy owl face the teeth of the winter wind and come away whole? How do we as a society force ourselves to address climate catastrophe?

"The future will be a product of our errors, hesitations and escapes," wrote Loren Eiseley in *The Night Country*. "The juggernaut of our civilization charges on, and we wait minutes, decades, centuries for the crash we have engendered."

The High Priestess knows that the cataclysm is coming and maybe all of the actions, words, and ideas in the world won't stop it. Maybe we all know it. What do we do in the meantime?

The High Priestess would have us reflect, turn inward to the dark to know ourselves.

III

THE EMPRESS

CHAPTER 3
DEATH AND REBIRTH

Is our world, then, the rotted corpse of a goddess? The very existence of life contains death, the destiny of every creature.
—Rachel Pollack, *Tarot Wisdom*

In the tarot tradition, many depictions of the Empress feature a woman surrounded by florid blooms and a field of golden grain, draped in luxurious cloth, eating pomegranate. The imagery calls to mind Aphrodite or Demeter, goddesses of harvest and plenty. Richness, beauty, comfort.

Yet the archetype of the Empress and her number, three, can call forth something different: creation, new growth, and renewal from death.

In the first week of March my three-year-old son and I hike into a floodplain forest looking for skunk cabbage—the first signs of spring in this part of the world.

Everything in the wet leafless wood is matted, sodden – the color of a road-killed possum—worn out from the winter. This is a difficult turning point in the year for wildlife, when the last of the dried berries and mast have run out, but the new growth hasn't yet started. Winter, while weak and exhausted, still lies cold and dank on the land.

But skunk cabbage, a strange and ancient denizen of shady swamps, overcomes the cold and celebrates the wetness.

The skunk cabbage generates its own heat, melting surrounding ice and snow. Blooming plants create a microclimate around its flowers that can be up to fifty degrees warmer than the surrounding soil and air.

The technical term is thermogenesis. A starch-filled underground stem fuels the metabolic heat production. Enzymes in the skunk cabbage alter the functions of its cells to convert stored energy into heat rather than growth.

In the early spring, the skunk cabbage seems almost more animal than plant.

"At air temperatures near freezing, a seemingly inactive skunk cabbage spadix is using oxygen and burning food at a rate nearly equal to that of a small shrew or hummingbird," writes biologist Roger Knutson in *Natural History* in 1979.

It breathes, it feeds on its energy reserves, it senses changes in weather and adjusts its internal temperature.

These are the first Ohio wildflowers to bloom each year, weeks before other spring woodland species.

In a low, wet spot in the woods, my son and I brush away the matted leaves and find a half-dozen reddish-purple spathes shooting out of the wet loam, fleshy teardrop-shaped hoods cupping a round yellow flower cluster called a spadix.

We drop down to our hands and knees, and dip our heads down to sniff the bulbous plants. The skunk cabbage reeks like rotten flesh. It produces two chemical compounds that account for the smell—skatole and cadaverine. Skatole is found in mammal feces; cadaverine in putrefying animal tissue.

Many of the insects that are active in the early spring and late winter scavenge carrion—beetles and flies seeking out dead animals that couldn't hold on through the long, cold season. The insects follow the scent into the skunk cabbage's meat-colored spathes and pollinate the plants by taking pollen from one plant to another.

The skunk cabbage is just one of many spring wildflowers to mimic the flesh of winter-killed animals, exemplifying the archetypical spring theme of death and rebirth. The bloody-looking flowers of red trillium, also called Wake Robin or Stinking Benjamin, have the "smell and appearance of raw beefsteak of uncertain age" writes Jack Sanders in *The Secrets of Wildflowers*, and it attracts green flesh flies found on garbage and roadkill. The small liver-colored flowers of wild ginger attract early spring flies and gnats that are looking for thawing carcasses of animals that died over the winter.

But the skunk cabbage is the first and uses its heating ability to get a jump on the competition for pollinators and sunlight.

The teardrop-shaped spathe is a fleshy leaf full of air pockets like an insulating Styrofoam. Inside the spathe, the plant maintains a temperature of seventy-two degrees around its round flower stalk.

My son and I peek inside the folds of the plant to view the flower. It feels prurient, this probing. The spadix is a pale, nude wrinkly mound studded with petal-less flowers.

The warm temperature attracts insects and helps to disperse the scent. The skunk cabbage can produce heat for up to two weeks. The plant consumes significant energy to maintain that temperature, but by blooming in late winter, the skunk cabbage can take advantage of sunlight on the forest floor before the trees leaf out in the spring.

As soon as the danger of frost has passed, the plant unfurls three-foot-long, one-foot-wide, tropical-looking leaves. This is often the first foliage available in the forest, but very few animals eat skunk cabbage. The leaves contain calcium olxalate crystals, a compound that causes burning and swelling in the mouth and throat.

By summer the large leaves will have withered and all that will be left aboveground of the skunk cabbage will be a slimy black stain and a seed ball that will be eaten by squirrels.

But belowground, the plant persists—and might survive indefinitely.

Rachel Lang in Penn State's biology department writes:

It is very difficult or even impossible to pull or even dig a skunk cabbage out of its soil foundation. The roots have circular surface ridges which grab onto the soil matrix and via root contractions actually help to pull the growing plant deeper and deeper into the soil system. Older plants, then, are rooted more deeply than younger plants. This contractile root adaptation may also help to prevent frost heaving of the plant out of the freezing and thawing wet soil matrix. The root system has been described as being "virtually indestructible" and may persist for decades and, possibly, even hundreds of years.

Specimens several hundred years old have been found. Researchers believe they can live thousands of years. The only limiting factor on a skunk cabbage's lifespan is the slow accretion of organic matter. As plants die and leaves fall, eventually the soil level rises and the wetland dries out.

Tarot cards are associated with the various elements: air, fire, water. The Empress is associated with earth. The skunk cabbage, like the Empress, is deeply rooted.

My son and I leave the skunk cabbage in the wet trough, and look for a higher, drier place in the sun. We lie down and feel cradled and supported. I tell him to close his eyes, to feel the earth pushing up, supporting our bodies.

I think about the poet Wendell Berry, who wrote, "My life is only the earth risen up a little way into the light, among the leaves."

Face down in a sunny patch of dirt, we smell the crumbled-up oak tannins. New research has discovered that soil microbes can enter the human body and boost the levels of serotonin and norepinephrine circulating in the systems, functioning as a natural antidepressant.

I need it, after the long winter with my young family.

"Every generation has to die in order that the next generation can come," writes Joseph Campbell in *The Power of Myth*. "As soon as you beget or give birth to a child, you are the dead one."

I look at my beautiful three-year old son, and know his life is paid for by mine and my wife's.

Many see something soft in the mother—I see something very different, having watched my wife bear and raise three young sons in quick succession. There is a tenacity and sacrifice, a willingness and strength to fight through exhaustion and nausea. To bear children you kill yourself.

This time of year, when the ground is still nearly frozen and the salamanders are walking over snow on soft bellies to vernal pools, crossing caustic salted roadways, to thaw and be clamped down upon, to soak in runoff, all to bring forth new life.

It is the Empress's ability to bear and withstand this struggle that allows her to bring new life into the world. It requires a sacrifice of oneself.

Every single aspect of our existence—every bite of food, drop of oil, molecule of breathable atmosphere—was built upon living organic web of life.

One of the things to reflect on for this card is gratitude. We live in a late-stage capitalistic hellscape, a socioeconomic system that perpetuates itself by creating dissatisfaction and unmet desires.

Meditating on gratitude will provide physical and psychological benefits. It's a good way to take care of yourself and the people you love.

THE EMPEROR

CHAPTER 4
FATHERS AND WARDENS

Late October—the last warm day of the year—I watched four fisheries biologists wade through a weedy slough, water splashing over the tops of their chest waders as they walked alongside a john boat to gather the nets for their aquatic sampling project.

If you stood on this shoreline of the western edge of Lake Erie 200 years ago and looked south, you would have stared at a marshland extending for miles. Now I could throw a rock across this largest contiguous pool leftover from what was once called the Great Black Swamp.

The Great Lakes are really a giant river, a massively complex flowing system of watersheds cycling toward the Atlantic. The water levels can fluctuate dramatically.

During high water, the Great Black Swamp became flooded forest and wetland habitat. In low water years, the shoreline receded and left behind upland forests and meadows.

The 4,800-square-mile quagmire was full of pests and predators and made travel difficult. So white settlers drained the land.

Ninety-five percent of Lake Erie's coastal wetlands were destroyed. The Cedar Point Wildlife Refuge preserved a tiny remnant of what was once a wetland the size of Connecticut.

The swamp was replaced with corn fields, which drain phosphorus into the Maumee River, fueling blooms of blue-green algae in Lake Erie that smother half the lake every summer and turn the water to poison.

The "algae" label is a misnomer—the gobs of green slime are actually a cyanobacteria. The organisms feed on agricultural runoff and secrete a toxin called microcystin that sickens people and animals. A massive bloom of bacteria captured national attention when it shut down the water supply for a half million people in Toledo in 2014.

According to climate researchers, warming temperatures and increased rainfall in the spring will further fuel the bacteria, extending the size and length of the blooms.

The Emperor card is associated with structure, fatherhood —a stern male ruler. The card's negative aspect is an old man, clinging to power, growing cruel and subverting his original intent to protect.

Previous generations conquered a massive swamp and walled off the shoreline in an effort to make life better. But our children will suffer for these ham-fisted triumphs over the water cycle.

The unintended consequence is that we may lose one of the most fecund lakes on the planet. Lake Erie makes up only 2 percent of the Great Lakes by water volume, but contains 50 percent of the fish.

The Great Black Swamp helped filter and process harmful nutrients before they entered the lake, but it also served as a nursery for one of the most productive freshwater fisheries in the world.

Many fish species need natural shorelines and marshy vegetated habitat to reproduce, and a protected place for young to survive past the fragile early stages of life. Almost all of Lake Erie's nearshore aquatic habitat has been destroyed to protect lake homes from erosion with the cycling water levels. Shallow areas had been dredged and the shoreline hardened with riprap, concrete, or sheet pile.

Even the last remnants of the coastal marshes are physically separated from the lake. We cling to the last vestige wetlands, isolating them to maintain water levels.

"We are trying to stabilize an unstable system," explains Matt Kovach, Lake Erie Coasts and Islands Program Manager with The Nature Conservancy. "We put the dikes there to keep the remaining marsh in the best shape we can."

Most of the wetlands' water control systems were designed and installed a century ago, primarily to preserve duck hunting opportunities. But now refuges all along the Great Lakes are removing old infrastructure and installing systems that will maintain water levels while reconnecting fish passages.

Tory Gabriel, a fisheries researcher and educator with Ohio Sea Grant, had brought me out to the marsh to check the nets in an effort to see what kind of fish are now recolonizing the wetland. We watched his team of grad students haul what looked like one hundred pounds of writhing fish to the edge of the shore.

The students pulled each individual fish from the net to measure and document size and species. Almost all of them were bowfin.

The biggest ones were the size and shape of a man's arm and were nearly impossible to hold. Incredibly powerful and covered in slime, they twisted out of the biologists' hands. The fish have heavy, bony skulls and an elongated dorsal fin that undulates like a snake.

The bowfin are the last species of an ancient order of fish that date back to the Jurassic period. They are reviled by anglers for mushy flesh, a mouth full of sharp teeth, and an unfounded reputation for harming gamefish populations. Anglers catch them and throw them on the banks.

Scientists do not pay them much attention. Fisheries research funding goes to glamour species. Study of bowfin is often incidental—as is the case here in Cedar Point Wildlife Refuge.

Yet, they are one of the most fascinating fish on the planet, and embody the best aspects of the Emperor: protective, self-sacrificing, essential.

Bowfin spawn in the spring. On Lake Erie, the fish move into nearshore, weedy habitat in April. A male and female pair up. The male creates a nest of matted vegetation, and females distribute the eggs.

Males fertilize eggs as they are released, and if the female doesn't leave after depositing the eggs, the male will chase her off. He will guard that nest aggressively, and then care for the young.

Solomon David, an aquatic ecologist at Michigan State University, is one of the few scientists studying bowfin and other primitive fishes. "Within the primitive fish group—sturgeons, paddlefish, gars, bowfin—parental care is unusual. The bowfin is the only one that does it," David says.

Wading in a shallow lake, David recalls coming upon a male bowfin on a nest, watching it flare its gills and open its mouth, to make it appear more intimidating. The fish was risking its life to fend off a much larger potential predator.

"Females invest energy by producing eggs," David says. "The males do not have an immediate physiological investment. The male's investment is making sure the next generation survives. Guarding the nest, rearing the young to three inches long, shepherding around hundreds if not a thousand of little bowfin —the males are not eating much. That is a significant investment. For the females, the investment is on the front end, the males it is on the back end."

The males herd the young-of-the-year into a bowfin ball, a swarming mass of little baby fish that the males guard voraciously.

Males will typically have a bright ocellus on their tail area—a highly visible black spot with a pale yellow ring. Females sometimes have the black spot. The young will also have the ocellus. Most scientists would say the eye spot pattern is a defense mechanism, a way to confuse predators to attack a bowfin's tail instead of its head.

But another theory is that the ocellus is a signal to help

young bowfin to home in on their father.

The young of the year fish are very fragile in the bowfin ball. David says that when young bowfin get collected for the aquarium trade, they die quickly without their fathers. The male bowfin is essential to its offspring's survival and success.

All morning, the scientists pull dozens of bowfin from the nets and record their length and weight before returning them to the water. Some of the fish weigh over ten pounds. It is a massive haul, and a great sign for the potential recovery of the lake.

"Bowfin are great indicators of restoration success," David says. "Having bowfin suggests that the marsh is healthy and will support a range of species. Biodiversity is critical to the resiliency of the entire ecosystem.

"We can reconnect the severed habitat, but we won't know if we are successful until frontier fish like the bowfin are found."

V

THE HIEROPHANT

CHAPTER 5
BLOOD TIES AND RITUAL

Off in the far northwestern corner of Ohio near the town of Hicksville, I sit on an aluminum ladder lashed to a tree in the predawn gloom. Fifteen feet up in the air, the wind cuts through the layers of camouflage and blaze orange clothing I wear just one day each year.

The tree-stand looks out over a spent cornfield owned by a family friend. My father hides somewhere behind me, in small woodlot of oak and hickory trees.

My stomach churns, having not enough sleep and no breakfast. I scan my surroundings, slow my breathing, listen closely to every sound.

My mind strains against the quiet. I feel fear, inadequacy, excitement, pleasure, boredom—the full range of human emotion.

I feel like a little boy, holding a too-heavy gun. It is as if I am reliving an initiation ritual that never took.

José Ortega y Gasset calls this state "mystical agitation" in *Meditations on Hunting*.

Even though I am not an avid hunter, the act of hunting sets my body into a hyperalert predatory trance.

This is the religion of my father, and so, reluctantly, it is also mine.

My father is a hard man to know. He projects a veneer of amiability and competence, but I have no idea how he feels about anything. The closest I can get to understanding his emotional core is to follow him into the woods with a gun.

Hunting is my father's defining characteristic. He reads all of the hunting magazines, attends banquets and auctions to benefit hunting organizations. His friends are all hunters. My boyhood home looked like a shrine to the fauna of North America, stuffed deer and elk staring down from the walls, flushed ducks and geese taking flight in my mother's living room.

When I was six years old, I received my hunter's safety card. We have hunted together nearly my whole life.

The Hierophant is the upholder of traditional teachings. This card traditionally depicts a high priest or pope addressing his acolytes. The Hierophant upholds the law, tradition, and dogma.

There are aspects of the Hierophant at play in the hunter—the requirement for orthodoxy, indoctrination, conformity.

Compare this character to that of the High Priestess. Whereas she embodies a spiritual knowledge and intuitive understanding, the Hierophant maintains tradition and expectations.

The card represents a power structure and authority—as well as the dark overtones of repression and persecution of those who will not conform to traditional values. It hints at the perversion of a power structure that has lost sight of the divine wonder that inspired the tradition in the first place.

I hate guns and only fire mine twice a year. Once to sight it in, and once to try to kill something. I reject trophy hunting and the culture of the hunting industry. And yet, I also see in hunting, a way to connect to the most ancient traditions of humanity and the broader community of the natural world.

I also see hunting as one of the only ways to understand and gain the approval of my father.

"We are always hunting something of our father's, and he's hunting too, and we're sure we'll know more of ourselves if we can get to him," writes Michael J. Meade.

As the sun rises and the deer start to move, shotguns fire in the distance from all directions. My anticipation builds.

From high up in the tree stand, I can hear them approaching from behind me on dry leaves: three does, two large and one smaller deer. The animals walk within fifty yards of where I sit and pause.

I draw my sights on the biggest one, hold my breath, and fire.

The bullet hits the doe in the upper shoulder, breaks the spine, and kills her before she hits the ground.

I watch with a sick feeling as the other two deer stare back at their dead companion. They seem to call and encourage her to get up, to come with them. Then they bound off, whistling a distress call, tails flying on high alert.

My father comes over to me from his tree, hugs me, and takes my gun.

I kneel and run my hands over the animal, touching the hide and feeling its warmth. There are precious few ritualized moments in my life, and this one is sacred.

I feel sadness for killing the animal. Then, I begin the long process of turning it into food, converting the landscape—the oak and hickory, corn and grass—into meat which would nourish my body and the bodies of my sons.

Only about 6 percent of our country's adult population hunts, according to survey data from the U.S. Fish and Wildlife Service. And yet, over 96 percent of the adult population eats meat.

So much of life is a cycle of organisms eating and being eaten, nutrients recombining and transforming. I barely register that I'm consuming living animals when I eat a cheeseburger. And yet, when it feeds my family this deer will remind me of my father, oak trees, and the November sunrise.

"Every day we foreclose one life over another, a never-ending triage, a constant choice of who will suffer so that we may live," writes Ted Kerasote in *Bloodties: Nature, Culture and the Hunt*. "Hunting attaches me to this place and the animals I love, asking me to own what each of us ought to own in some personal way—the pain that runs the world."

My three boys and I will eat this deer, saving money this winter and avoiding factory-raised protein stuffed with antibiotics. But I also feel good about the kill because it is beneficial to the environment.

White-tailed deer were nearly extirpated in Ohio 100 years ago, but with the systemic killing of predators and hunting regulations the deer bounced back.

Today there are thirty million deer in the American forests and suburbs, 100 times more animals than a century ago.

Whitetails thrive in what's called "edge habitat"—a patchwork of young regenerating forests and open grass. The Rust Belt's flight to suburbia turned the landscape into a deer paradise.

The entire Eastern Forest ecosystem is reeling from the devastating effects of deer overpopulation.

"White-tailed deer likely impact every landscape east of the Mississippi River. The damage has been insidious—both slow moving and cumulative. Unfortunately, the harm is often overlooked, or worse, accepted as somehow natural," writes The Nature Conservancy. "In our opinion, no other threat to forested habitats is greater at this point in time—not lack of fire, not habitat conversion, not climate change. Only invasive exotic insects and disease have been comparable in magnitude."

The deer are responsible for widespread declines in songbirds, moths, wildflowers, and uncounted other species. I've seen the damage firsthand, in springtime forests where diverse native plants grow only in isolated pens, fenced off from the ravenous herd.

Jim Bissell, curator of botany and director of natural areas at the Cleveland Museum of Natural History said preserving biodiversity "Is all about managing deer. You shouldn't be able to see through a forest in Northeast Ohio because of the dense understory of shrubs saplings and herbaceous plants. Wood warbler, wood thrush, hooded warbler, ovenbird all nest in that habitat. We hunt [deer] on our natural areas because once the native plants crash, it's hard to bring the diversity back."

In a world where so many animals are facing diminishing resources, killing whitetail deer isn't just acceptable, but preferable.

"A thing is right," wrote Aldo Leopold in *A Sand County Almanac*, "when it preserves the integrity, stability, and beauty of the biotic community. It is wrong when it tends otherwise."

There are three times as many deer in the woods as there are hunters in the United States. Somebody has to do it.

VI

THE LOVERS

CHAPTER 6
TILL DEATH

At the Cleveland Museum of Natural History's outdoor wildlife exhibit, a four-foot-tall, male sandhill crane named Niles stares intently at Michelle Leighty, Manager of Wildlife Resources at the museum.

Niles is too tame to be released. Wildlife rehabilitators found him wandering the parking lot of a truck stop in Michigan, picking bugs off car radiators.

Leighty suspects Niles imprinted on humans as a juvenile. There is a period in a young bird's development where it observes its parents (or a surrogate) to determine its identity. Niles thinks he is human.

In the wild, a human-imprinted crane may not survive. It has no fear of people—which is not to say it is tame, in fact human imprinted birds can be abnormally aggressive as territorial instincts are triggered by humans rather than others of their species.

But Niles seems to like his caretaker. Leighty feeds the cranes, provides stimulus to keep them active, trains the animals to help the museum staff with their care.

Niles presses against the mesh of the cage and pokes his huge, sharp bill through the wire. He almost seems like a dog, happy to see its owner.

We walk around to the back of the enclosure, where the staff only can go. The female crane, named Daphne, approaches us.

A fist-sized egg lies in the dirt a few feet away, the pair's first mating attempt. Normally, the cranes are inquisitive and playful with their caretakers. But now Leighty carries a trash can lid as a shield when she enters the enclosure for care and feeding.

As we get closer to the makeshift nest, the cranes stand together and throw back their heads, extending their elongated tracheas, and start to screech. The sound is deafening, a prehistoric alarm.

The birds perform the unison call as part of pair bonding, but also use it to threaten predators. I imagine a fox trying to steal a hatchling would die of fright if it heard this sound at close range.

The pair have been housed together for several years, but this is the first year they had mated. Leighty found an egg smashed in a corner of the cage a week ago. This second egg also would never hatch.

Leighty had entered the enclosure and shaken it. The museum doesn't have a permit to breed cranes. But Leighty leaves the egg in the makeshift nest. If she takes it, the female may lay another and deplete her calcium and other nutrients.

The pair had performed a dancing ritual in the spring, an involved display with jumping and flapping, swordplay with the long beaks.

Leighty said Niles wasn't very good. He mostly watched the wilder female dance while he stood off to the side looking confused. Human-imprinted birds often have difficulty communicating with their own species.

I imagine Niles as a sullen boy at a high school dance, watching girls on the dance floor; or as a feckless lover, disappointing his wife.

Cranes are often said to mate for life. While the phrase sounds romantic, reality is more prosaic.

Research on sandhill cranes suggests that if a pair fails to produce young after a few attempts, they will likely divorce. And upon the death of a mate, the surviving crane connects with a new partner within a few days.

The scientific term "perennial monogamy" feels more apt.

Yet many bird species tend toward long-term monogamous relationships, more so than other animal species. What is it about birds in general, and cranes specifically, that favors long-term committed partnership?

"With many birds, males and females have equal parental duties," explains crane researcher Matt Hayes. "Male and female birds form bonds and reaffirm them to successfully raise and protect offspring. With mammals, the females carry the young to term in utero, females supply lactation, they do the bulk of the work. Most reptiles and fish do not provide much parental care. Birds are this unique class. When males and females work together to defend the clutch and provide resources they have higher reproductive success.

"I don't want to anthropomorphize, but my experience with cranes suggests there is something more going on beyond reproduction. Pairs like to hang out with each other, more than with other cranes. They've got a lot invested in each other."

Cranes only raise two offspring per year, and they have to protect, feed, and teach their young in order to survive. It is a slow, difficult process to ensure the next generation of cranes survives.

Sandhill crane populations have slowly been rebounding in Ohio after being wiped out in the late 1920s from wetland loss and overhunting.

"We haven't done any active management—they've been coming back on their own," explains Dr. Laura Kearns, a wildlife biologist with the Ohio Department of Natural Resources. "In Ohio we've only documented around 50 breeding pairs. Our numbers are much lower compared to the rest of the Midwest. The bulk of the population is in Michigan, Minnesota, and Ontario."

The first breeding pair of sandhill cranes after the extirpation were found in the Killbuck Valley, a sprawling wetland in Ohio's Amish country, in 1985. There is a bike trail through the countryside that runs along the wetlands in this area, and it was here that I first encountered wild cranes.

Prior to the nesting period, sandhill cranes paint their plumage by pulling up rotten vegetation and mud with their bills and staining their feathers. The activity turns their gray plumage to a brown color that matches the color of the dead grass in nesting areas. But the red skin on their foreheads stands out against the pale gray plumage.

I'd spotted a pair of cranes across the marsh, and took some photos with a telescopic lens. When I pulled the files off the camera, I noticed that each crane had a young, camouflaged colt following it. Cranes often lay two eggs, a few days apart. After hatching, the older chick is more aggressive than the younger, and the two must be separated by the parents. The parents will split up and walk in separate directions so that one chick will follow one parent and the other chick the other parent.

I think about my wife and how we are constantly separating our three young boys.

Nearly all our resources and energy are put toward their wellbeing. It often feels like we are no longer lovers, but partners providing for our offsprings' needs. What brought us together? Attraction. Biology. What keeps us together is obligation for what we've created. Potentially, more biology.

The cranes reflect aspects of the Lovers card.

There are two historical variants of this trump which have almost opposite themes. One interpretation suggests love is a choice we make—the other a lack of choice, to be swept up by forces larger than ourselves.

In the Tarot of Marseille, the Lovers card features a man standing between two women, some suggest symbolizing a choice between virtue and vice.

In many cases, wild sandhill cranes will form trios after the nesting period. An experienced male and female pair will be joined by an unpaired female. Occasionally the male chooses the interloper.

In the Visconti-Sforza tarot, the card depicts a man and woman clasping hands, standing under a blindfolded angel. Love is blind, and dictated by fate, divine or profane forces beyond our control.

It is the latter interpretation that applies to the captive cranes, bound together by circumstance and wire mesh, driven to union by their biology.

I imagine most long-term relationships feel like some combination of those themes—the initial infatuation, preference, choice; the cementing of that choice in intertwined lives, and our hopes that we made the right choice as time goes on.

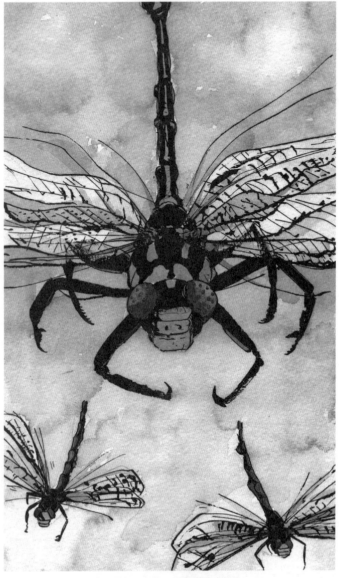

THE CHARIOT

CHAPTER 7
THE DRAGONHUNTER

On an idyllic early August afternoon on the Grand River near Harpersfield, Ohio, a huge dragonfly zigzags over a riverbend, dipping its tail into the water, depositing eggs.

Its thick, black body is decorated with stripes shaped like golden spears and arrows. At nearly three and a half inches long, it is a giant of the dragonfly world.

The dragonhunter (*Hagenius brevistylus*), as its name implies, feeds on dragonflies. It captures insects in midair with powerful legs and devours prey nearly its own size. They have a reputation for being fearless.

Naturalists have witnessed them chasing birds. There are scientific illustrations showing dragonhunters clasping killed hummingbirds. Experts are skeptical regarding a dragonhunter's ability to take down avian prey, but to even consider it speaks to the species' ferocity and power.

The dying mother dragonfly is nearly broken. Its large green compound eyes have been gouged, its head punctured, thorax cracked and leaking ichor.

Dragonfly mating is brutal. Males clasp females tightly around the head, oftentimes piercing the exoskeleton with the spines on the legs. The pair will land in a tree and the male first tries to gouge out any competing males' sperm with its sex organs, then it will deposit its own sperm. The last male to copulate with the female before she lays the eggs has the best chance to breed successfully.

Biologists have determined nearly all female dragonflies in the clubtail family suffer serious injuries during mating. The male dragonhunter inflicts more severe damage on its mate than any other dragonfly.

Soon after mating, the female expels her eggs over the river. The untended offspring scatter and drift apart in the current. They fall to the bottom and are soon covered in silt. Two weeks later, larval dragonhunters emerge.

So begins the difficult life of a predaceous insect, constantly feeding and avoiding being eaten. In this aquatic phase, the dragonfly is called a nymph or naiad.

The dragonhunter nymph is the color and shape of a rotting leaf—a dark, oval disc with six sprawling legs. Its head is equipped with projectile piercing mouthparts for snaring prey, which it shoots out from below its face. For up to seven years, dragonhunter nymphs will prowl the river, seeking out vulnerable animals to snatch up and consume, including other dragonfly nymphs, tadpoles, and even small fish.

The immature insect must survive winter freezes, spring run-off, and hungry smallmouth bass. It will hide under riverbed stones, stalk caddisfly larvae, and shed five exoskeletons before it emerges from the water to metamorphize into a completely different form.

Driven by instinct and weather conditions, a group of nymphs will crawl out of the river under the cover of darkness, climb up a vertical surface, and begin the difficult process of breaking out of their exoskeletons. Not all of the dragonflies will metamorphize successfully—some emerge bent, broken. Only the strongest and luckiest survive the ordeal.

Imagine what it must feel like, to slough off the rigid structure that has held you together your entire life. You wriggle and pulsate within your husk, and then crack it open, emerging soft and crumpled like wet laundry. You must expand and stretch, pulling yourself free of your brittle former body. And then you must pump bodily fluids and air into your new form, stretching out like a balloon, before your body hardens into some misshapen thing.

Teneral, or newly emerged, dragonhunters are bright green and soft. During this fragile state—before the wings and exoskeleton harden, the dragonflies are defenseless. This process usually occurs overnight to try to avoid most avian predators.

By dawn, the successful dragonhunters can start to fly.

For the next three months, the adult dragonhunter will be one of the dominant species in its environment. It will attack large prey items from above, flying at speeds of up to twenty-five miles per hour, knocking insects out of midair. They feed on ebony jewelwings, river cruisers, swallowtail butterflies, and even monarch butterflies.

After two weeks on the wing, the adult dragonhunters will sexually mature and begin the process of mating and egg laying all over again.

A new generation of tiny insects will be cast off into the river to fend for themselves. The weak will be eaten. The lucky will hold dominion after years of struggle.

The divinatory meanings of the Chariot portend success, victory, the defeat of enemies in battle. It can represent someone who has overcome obstacles to achieve a goal through will, tenacity, and competitiveness. The Chariot represents forward motion.

The traditional representation of the Chariot depicts a conquering king, riding in a four-cornered carriage pulled by sphinxes or horses.

The king is powerful, but also fortunate—lucky. He doesn't hold the reins of his carriage. In fact, the animals pulling the chariot are often illustrated as pulling in opposing directions. The king is carried forward by circumstance.

Despite being a land vehicle, the card is associated with water. The card's rushing momentum mirrors the large rivers where the dragonhunter thrives.

There are other echoes between the dragonfly and the traditional representation of this card.

A Dazzle of Dragonflies, by Forrest L. Mitchell and James L. Lasswell, explores the historical and cultural significance of these insects. The authors explain that the most common animal referenced in colloquial names for dragonflies in Europe is the horse: Devil's Horse in Romania, Witch's Horse in Finland and France. Germans have a phrase, the Pferd und Wagen, horse and wagon. Also, in Japan, the dragonfly was historically known as katsumushi (the invincible insect), a favorite symbol of strength among Japanese warriors.

The concept of success or victory after long struggle is also reflected in the natural history of dragonflies. "Odonates [dragonflies and damselflies] lived 200 million years ago, alongside Jurassic dinosaurs. And insects not so very different from them where flying 100 million years before that," writes Jill Silsby in *Dragonflies of the World*.

))●(((

Dragonflies have survived for so long in their current form because they are highly successful predators. But this long-term viability is also due to their ability to disperse across huge distances to find new habitats. This has helped them survive for hundreds of millions of years, to ride out climatic and other environmental shifts.

The dragonhunter specifically has thrived for so long that when it evolved, the planet's continents were jammed together in single landmass called Pangea. The dragonhunter is the only species of its genus in North America, and its nearest relatives are in Asia – separated by millions of years of continental drift.

While triumph is the overriding message of this card, it has dark undercurrents. What motivates the charioteer to compete and dominate others?

It is the fear of death, an inability to face mortality. Throughout a dragonfly's life it is always the hunter and the hunted. In one of my favorite tarot decks, by Herman Haindl, the charioteer is on fire and is chased by a giant boar-wolf-god. The driver is hunted by his mortality. Achieving success is the only way to stave off nothingness. But that victory can be hollow.

As Rachel Pollack writes, despite overcoming life's challenges, the charioteer knows "nothing at all about the ultimate truth of oneself and the cosmos." The conquering warrior persona is often a mask, like an exoskeleton of armor. Without it, the charioteer is formless.

In our culture, dominated by massive income inequality, cruel political leaders, and militarized racist police, we find ourselves facing the dark side of the Chariot. It is hard not to anthropomorphize the dragonhunter that kills everything it can catch and enacts sexual violence on its mates.

But we must keep in mind the cards that are still to come—Strength, Justice, and Temperance. And also, the Tower, which portends the annihilation of structures built by would-be Charioteers.

VIII

STRENGTH

CHAPTER 8
SKY RIVER RUNS TWO WAYS

The lakefront is where the corroded industrial heart of Cleveland still beats.

On the west bank of the mouth of the Cuyahoga River, machines load rock salt onto railcars.

Companies mine salt deposits from an ancient sea, 1,800 feet below Lake Erie. The salt is shipped to other rusting northern towns to de-ice the roads in winter.

In the harbor, massive freighters offload taconite pellets, brown chunks of low-grade ore from Lake Superior's Iron Range to feed the steel mills.

Just offshore, Army Corps of Engineers construction teams float heavy equipment on barges out onto the lake to repair the concrete breakwater, shielding the city from the worst of the coming winter storms.

All of it represents an effort to dominate the land through brute force, to reshape nature to our whim.

By accident or design, a stand of sumac and cottonwood trees grows on this industrial waterfront—bordered by concrete, rusting railways, and piles of rock gouged from the earth.

Wendy Park, just twenty-two acres of greenspace, supports 260 species of birds, and migrating monarch butterflies. The woodlot provides a place for animals to rest and refuel after crossing the huge expanse of a Great Lake.

On a Sunday morning in early September, around 4,000 monarch butterflies blanket the trees. Branches are dripping with bright orange and black insects clumsily clinging to the leaves.

The day before, these insects had been crossing Lake Erie from Canada ahead of a cold front.

These butterflies had likely been born in Ontario a few weeks earlier, and were now on their journey south, crossing more than 2,000 miles to get to the monarch overwintering sites in the mountain forests of central Mexico.

Monarchs travel singularly, covering from 50 to 100 miles during the daylight hours. At night, the insects cluster in large groups called roosts. This huge group had converged on Wendy Park to wait out rain and high winds.

As soon as the temperature and the winds favored their departure, they would continue onward. But on this Sunday morning, I ran through the trees with my sons, necks craned to look up into the fluttering orange spectacle.

Lake Erie is the most developed of all the Great Lakes. Nearly all the woodlands and wetlands have been converted to something more convenient for human use. With so little habitat left, places like Wendy Park are tenuous links in a chain spanning thousands of miles.

The tiny park nestled in the industrial landscape, surrounded by broken and reshaped rock and metal, reflects nature's persistence. The butterflies, battered by the wind and rains, find refuge in this industrial landscape so that they can carry their next generation of monarchs forward.

The nature of Strength as it relates to tarot is the capacity to persist. In some tarot decks, Strength is instead called Fortitude – resilience in the face of pain and adversity.

Most traditional depictions of Strength feature a woman pressing shut the open mouth of an ornery male lion. To get this card in a reading suggests that the querent will have to do something that is not easy but necessary—a task that requires self-discipline and strength of mind.

While so much human energy is used to reshape the world, Strength encourages us to master ourselves.

Historically, Strength was associated with subduing sexual desire. This echoes the behavior of the monarch butterfly, which delays its mating activity to enable its journey to Mexico.

The technical term is diapause. By shutting off reproduction, northern-born monarch butterflies modify their bodies and life spans. Instead of living for a few weeks, a migrant monarch may live up to ten months. Nutrients are shifted from reproduction to flight muscles and energy storage. All of the animal's resources are directed toward surviving the journey and overwintering.

Author and lepidopterist Robert Michael Pyle compares the monarch's journey to a sky river that runs two ways, "North with the spring, south with the fall… This is a current that changes direction with the season, a tide with a turnaround time of six months instead of six hours."

Migrating monarchs arrive in the oyamel mountain forest of central Mexico around the first week of November. There they congregate in massive hordes, millions of insects bending the tree branches where they gather. They huddle in orange masses to endure cold temperatures and snow, sometimes feeding on whatever sustenance they can find near the roosts, but mostly they conserve their energy.

Come spring, the roosts break up. The aged, tattered butterflies travel as far north as their wings can carry them and start their delayed breeding process. They seek out newly emerging patches of milkweed.

The various milkweed species are the only plants that monarch caterpillars feed on, providing a natural predator repellent. Plants in the milkweed family defend themselves against insects by producing noxious chemicals called cardiac glycosides. Most insects avoid milkweeds, but monarchs and a few other insect species specialize in processing the toxic compounds.

Monarchs use the chemicals to their advantage – the milkweed's defenses are absorbed and carried forward by monarch caterpillars and butterflies. To eat one would sicken many predators. The monarch's bold coloration is an advertisement to predators that they are poisonous.

Newly hatched monarchs grow from tiny grubs less than a tenth of an inch to pinky-finger-sized caterpillars 3,000 times their hatching weight in a period of about two weeks. They are voracious and fast growing. This appetite drives the monarchs continually northward, each subsequent generation seeking fresh patches of milkweed to colonize.

By the time the monarch butterflies arrive in the northern part of their range in Ohio, they might be the great-great-grandkids of the butterflies that had arrived the year before. The migration is a sequential, multigenerational relay race.

The monarch butterfly perfectly juxtaposes resiliency and vulnerability. It struggles against extreme temperatures, the vagaries of the wind and other weather disturbances. It seeks food plants that might be cleared by development, or covered in herbicides or pesticides from farming. And if it survives the massive journey spanning a continent, it can only hope its roosting sites are still intact.

As with so many migratory species relying on a network of distributed habitats across multiple geographies, cultures, and regulatory regimes—these interdependent, finely tuned systems tying the continent together are fraying.

Experts estimate that the eastern population of monarchs has diminished by 90 percent over the past twenty years.

So many species are facing gradual decline due to habitat loss from human development, but few face a situation as precarious as the monarch. The monarchs spend the winter in just a handful of mountaintops in Mexico's Sierra Madre range where the oyamel fir trees protect the butterflies from freezing rain and snow, holding in the warmth.

Lepidopterists estimate a billion monarchs overwintered in this region twenty-five years ago, but less than 33 million inhabit the dwindling oyamel fir forests today. Many areas are protected, but illegal subsistence logging has damaged the remaining forests. And climate change is making the situation worse.

Ecologists predict less than a three-degree temperature rise over pre-industrial levels would destroy around 70 percent of the existing oyamel fir forest habitat by 2030. By the end of this century, the climate models suggest that oyamel firs could no longer grow in the preserve at all.

Forestry biologists are planting oyamel firs at higher altitudes to meet the coming climatic shifts, but struggle to adapt seedlings to colder locations with thin soil.

I think of the people struggling to save the monarch butterfly, and specifically this amazing migratory phenomenon, and it reminds me of a quote from Viktor Frankl's, *Man's Search for Meaning*.

"The transitoriness of our existence in no way makes it meaningless. But it does constitute our responsibleness… At any moment, man must decide, for better or for worse, what will be the monument of his existence."

All of us are facing nearly insurmountable odds against a warming climate, the momentum of Anthropocene extinction. We can feel powerless against so much suffering and loss to come.

And yet, Strength tells us to focus on what it is that we want to accomplish that would make this transitory existence meaningful.

THE HERMIT

CHAPTER 9
OLD MAN IN THE WOODS

On the side of the road in the Wayne National Forest, down the street from the state prison, my son and I met Marcel Weiand and Ryan Wagner, researchers studying eastern box turtle populations in Southeast Ohio.

Weiand is a biology graduate student at Ohio University and Wagner an undergrad field technician.

The four of us hiked into the warm deciduous woods that summer morning with our turtle tracking equipment.

Wagner carried what looks like an old rooftop TV antenna to listen for the signals coming from previously captured, radio-tagged study turtles.

As we walked, he listened intently through his headphones for chirps while waving the arm-length antenna around the woods.

The signal gets louder as Wagner gets closer to the transmitter—an inch-long box with a battery and a six-inch antenna—epoxied to each study turtle's shell.

But the hilly terrain can bounce the signal in odd angles, driving the seeker in circles, through brambles, up and down ravines. Even if it is a few inches away, a hiding box turtle can be difficult to spot.

Like any respectable hermit wandering the gothic Appalachian forests, these box turtles did not want to be found.

In early May, Weiand had hired a tracker with specially trained Boykin Spaniels to find as many box turtles as possible in a study area.

A team of human researchers could spend hours trying to find a single turtle in the woods unaided, whereas the dogs, using scent, can round up dozens in a session—sniffing turtles out of the woods and then carrying them back to their trainer gently in their mouths.

Weiand and Wagner fastened radio transmitters to the shells of thirty captured turtles, and released them back into the study area. Every morning, the researchers would go out and track the movement of the individual animals, recording GPS location, temperature, soil moisture, and other information to study the turtles' use of the landscape.

As the experiment progressed, they would find new turtles to document. They had identified over 100 individual animals in a few months.

The purpose of the study was twofold, to gather detailed data on how eastern box turtles use the various habitats in their environment; and to determine, if possible, how a new major road cutting through the forested hills would impact these animals. The study would last two years.

So far, the results varied. Some turtles wandered, while others were homebodies.

Box turtles by nature are of the earth. They often dig a shallow depression in the dirt called a form and slide their backsides into the soil to sit and watch the world around them. They may stay in their form for hours or even days if the weather is too hot or too cold.

While they may sit still for long periods, C. Kenneth Dodd, in *North American Box Turtles: A Natural History*, suggests these turtles have some degree of an "inner, psychic life."

Box turtles recognize the features of their landscape, notice our comings and goings, and have a sense of place. Even while stationary, they are alert and perceptive.

"It is hard to shake the impression that box turtles are

somehow much better than we are at economy of activity, leaving ample time for contemplation," writes Dodd.

Despite the sedentary reputation, research shows that the turtles are actively using large areas of habitat, moving around to favorable places to feed, mate, or nest.

"I don't think people understand how much depth there is to what they do," Weiand says. "When people see a turtle, it's usually inside its shell. But they move a lot. They travel for mating, foraging, overwintering, or laying eggs."

Also, some turtles just rove.

"It has long been suspected that certain box turtles do not settle into a home range but seem to wander randomly over a pathway known only to themselves. Evidence suggests that such animals do not retrace their routes and hence are true transients," writes Dodd.

These wandering nomads likely serve a function of promoting genetic diversity by traveling to populations outside of their immediate vicinity.

While transients are loners, most box turtles are not.

"They're incredibly social creatures. The data shows five out of six turtles we find are with other turtles," Weiand said. Sometimes Weiand finds a pair copulating, other times the turtles are amiably standing together as if in conversation.

These reptiles have a long time to form communities with their neighbors.

Turtles are among the longest-lived of all vertebrates. Box turtles found in the Northeastern U.S. have been dated at 138 years old. And box turtles exceeding 100 years of age are probably not rare.

This longevity makes it difficult to study box turtle population dynamics—an individual study animal could likely outlive its observer. A population of adults could persist for decades while subtle changes in the ecosystem prevent them from producing successful offspring. The population would seem to vanish without any explanation or way to recover.

Box turtles are in decline—they are listed as a "species of concern" in Ohio.

"Although it has never been adequately quantified, the loss or alteration of habitat is probably the greatest threat to the continued existence of box turtles," wrote Dodd. "Given the extent of habitat loss, it is surprising that box turtles have survived in some of the enclaves where they have, but it is unlikely that they will continue to do so much longer as human populations explode and mindless consumption drives the society."

Like the Hermit—box turtles need to get away from us.

So much human activity creates what's called edge habitat—carving up contiguous woodlands and swamps into smaller parcels bounded by developments or parklands. The edge is where the roads are. Thousands of turtles are killed by cars each year. The edge is also where some predators thrive—domestic dogs and raccoons are box turtle killers.

With the slow reproductive rate, the loss of even a few adults out of a population can be devastating over a long term. I worry that there may not be many wild box turtles around for my son's generation, and even fewer left for his children.

Also, studies show box turtles decline on protected preserves where people are present. The physical disturbance associated with human activities has a negative impact on the population, even if all the habitat needs are met.

Box turtles just want to be left alone, like the Hermit. They aren't antisocial, they have just chosen another path. They need room.

On a steep slope covered in dry fallen oak leaves, Wagner finds a big male turtle that may be older than anyone in our party.

My eight-year-old son gingerly picks it up with both hands. It is one of the more congenial study subjects. Instead of withdrawing into its shell, the handsome yellow and black turtle looks at my son with its red eyes, friendly and willing to engage. It is patient, curious, and gentle.

In *Jung and Tarot: An Archetypal Journey*, author Sallie Nichols suggests the Hermit reappears at the time when we most need him to shed light upon contemporary problems.

"One look into the kind eyes of this old monk tells us that he has not trudged painfully down the centuries to preach to us or berate us for wrongdoing," Nichols writes.

In tarot tradition, the Hermit drops out of the superficial activities of society to reckon with the important issues facing humanity. While he is most comfortable alone, the lantern he carries also provides light for others to see. The Hermit transitions in and out of isolation to share his knowledge.

I wonder what my son will remember of this day when he is older, and what wisdom the turtle might have imparted.

X

WHEEL *of* FORTUNE

CHAPTER 10
THE FIRMAMENT OF TIME

Wheel of Fortune is a difficult card to interpret, as it "tells of a turn of events the person cannot control or even rationally predict. " So writes Rachel Pollack in *The Complete Illustrated Guide to Tarot*.

The traditional meaning of this card is to note life's disruption—a turn is coming. But how long is the cycle of the wheel, and where are we on it? Will we still be on the wheel when it circles back to the top, or will we be ground underneath?

When I see this card, I can't help but think of fallen giants.

In the Kirtland Hall of Prehistoric Life at the Cleveland Museum of Natural History, the fossilized skull of a 365-million-year-old apex predator gapes menacingly at visitors.

The heavy jaws and bony plates belong to *Dunkleosteus terrelli*, the largest of a line of armored fishes that went extinct at the end of the Devonian Period, or "The Age of Fishes."

They grew to twenty feet long and could weigh over a ton. The shearing jaws look like they could snap a grown person in half.

Paleontologists estimate those terrible jaws had a bite force of 80,000 pounds per square inch, one of most powerful bites in the world.

"*Dunkleosteus terrelli* was the largest living vertebrate in its time," says Bill Havlin, former associate curator of vertebrate paleontology at the Cleveland Museum of Natural History "And there were lots of them. We know from the amount of remains we find in a small area, they were very prolific. You wouldn't want to be on a boat in the Devonian sea. You'd be gone in a minute."

Half a lifetime ago, Hlavin studied Devonian fish under the former museum curator David Dunkle, after whom Dunkleosteus was named in 1956.

When Hlavin was working on his doctoral dissertation, he looked at every specimen of Devonian armored fish found around the globe. "After looking at all those specimens, I can unequivocally say that the collections at the Cleveland Museum of Natural History are the finest collections in the world."

Three hundred and sixty five million years ago Northeast Ohio was under seawater.

"It's hard to grasp the concept of 365 million years ago," says Glenn Storrs, curator of vertebrate paleontology at the Cincinnati Museum Center. "People try to put the geologic timescale into context using clocks and distances as analogies. The presence of humans in the history of the planet occurs in the last second of a twenty-four-hour clock. These fish are ten minutes to the hour."

The climate was warmer during the Devonian—the polar ice caps had melted, and a shallow "epi-continental" sea covered the low-lying areas of North America.

A portion of the North American continent was rising at that time and rivers were draining sediment into the sea, creating a muddy runoff. This mud layer had accumulated to produce a soft sea bottom, and when animals died their bodies sunk into the muck and were buried quickly.

In most marine environments, dead animals rot. Aerobic bacteria destroy cartilage and soft tissues, and ocean currents disperse the skeleton.

But on the nearly lifeless sea floor around Cleveland, there were no scavengers or bacteria to feed on animals that died and drifted down to the bottom.

"Organic material didn't deteriorate in this anoxic environment," Storrs says "It's great for preserving fossils."

That thick layer of ooze eventually formed what's known as

the Cleveland Shale, a flaky, black sedimentary stone that stretches across northern Ohio.

The fossils found in the Cleveland Shale, especially of the sharks from that time period, preserve an incredible level of detail, including body outlines, impressions of skin textures and soft tissues.

Devonian fish and sharks lived all over the planet's oceans. But Cleveland happens to have the world's best-preserved specimens. The fossilized bones of Devonian fish and sharks are still falling out of the eroding black cliffs along the Rocky River today.

"There are at least forty different species of fish found in the Cleveland shale, but naturally *Dunkleosteus terrelli* was the king," Hlavin says. "Why so big? There are all kinds of theories as to why—favorable temperatures of the oceans, lots of oxygen in the water, a tremendous food supply."

But it's hard to stay on top. Eventually Dunkleosteus and the entire order of armored fish went extinct, while sharks survived.

"Maybe the Arthrodires became too top heavy with their armored heads. The sharks were sleeker and faster," Hlavin says. "The sharks were incredibly smooth and simple, and they really haven't changed much through time."

Thinking about extinctions causes us to confront anxieties too big to name.

What kind of benevolent personal God would spend hundreds of millions of years tinkering with sea monsters doomed to extinction?

We've been wrestling with this question for decades.

"The hint of extinction in the geological past was a cold wind out of a dark cellar. It chilled men's souls," writes Loren Eiseley in *The Firmament of Time*, published in 1960. "A vast and shadowy history loomed in the rocks. It threatened to be a history in which man's entire destiny would lose the significance he had always attached to it."

Even today, most of us have a distorted perception of evolution and speciation—it's baked into the very iconography of the tree of life. We have this view that nature builds and branches toward ever increasing diversity and complexity—upward and outward. But that view is barely more accurate than the medieval era's Great Chain of Being.

More than 99 percent of all species that ever lived on Earth have disappeared.

"Life is a copiously branching bush, continually pruned by the grim reaper of extinction, not a ladder of predictable progress," writes biologist Stephen J. Gould in *Wonderful Life*. "As Freud observed, our relationship with science must be paradoxical because we are forced to pay an almost intolerable price for each major gain in knowledge and power—the psychological cost of progressive dethronement from the center of things, and increasing marginality in an uncaring universe."

The enormity of time and the seeming randomness of the spectacle of life cause us to question whether life has any meaning, to wonder if any God is there at all.

"Nature is known to have created a multitude of forms before the present, played with them, building armor and strange reptilian pleasures, only to let them pass like discarded toys on a playroom floor," writes Eiseley.

The concept of the Wheel of Fortune goes back to the Babylonians, the idea that fate is capricious and random, that those on top will inevitably be ground under the wheel in time.

The Wheel was widely used in the Middle Ages to show the downfall of the mighty, and to promise the devout and downtrodden that they may rise to a heavenly reward.

But it will not stop there, but rather continue its seemingly senseless pattern of birth and decay.

In *Jung and Tarot: An Archetypal Journey*, Sallie Nichols

takes a critical look at the Tarot of Marseille imagery. Typhon, a monkey-headed Egyptian god, is depicted on his way down. He appears to plead with the viewer. The other being, Anubis, is on his way back to the top of the circle. They seem to be strapped to the wheel, like all of us, against our will.

"Whatever power commands Fortune's Wheel, it is evidently amoral," writes Nichols.

Change is the only constant. Any sense of permanence is an illusion of our limited perspective and lifespan. This is the message of the Wheel of Fortune.

So as we are helplessly trapped to the senseless grinding wheel, where do we turn? Possibly to other traditions.

I think about the Tibetan Buddhist sand mandalas representing the Kalachakra (wheel of time). During eleven days of meditation and ritual, a group of monks construct an incredibly complex image from painted sand, layered with meanings. At the end of the practice, the monks sweep the mandala away.

Often Western onlookers view the dismantling of the mandala with shock and horror at its destruction.

But to the monks, the dismantling is sacred as the construction. The deities invoked are asked to return to their sacred homes, and the painted sand is poured into local waters.

At the center of this process is the motivation of altruism – the monks would have us try to let go of attachment, and instead emphasize compassion for all other life.

The wheel turns for all of us, naked upright apes and giant armored fish alike.

XI

JUSTICE

CHAPTER 11
BALANCING THE SCALES

It stared at me from the backyard, appearing overnight.

A huge globular tumor had reared up out of the earth, white like the belly of a rotting fish, or the crown of a skull emerging from a hastily dug grave.

A giant puffball mushroom (*Calvatia gigantean*) had emerged at the woods edge.

Fear of mushrooms, or mycophobia, stems from the risk of accidentally consuming deadly poisonous species. But many people feel a low-grade loathing or disgust for fungi, associated with molds, decay, and rot.

As mycologist Paul Stamets writes in *Mycelium Running*, "Fungi are the interface organisms between life and death."

More animal than plant, the fungi share a common ancestor with the animal kingdom, splitting off from our simple forbears some 1.1 billion years ago. Fungi obtain nourishment by digesting other organisms. They hunt, parasitize, and scavenge.

We know so little about fungi, but they undergird the very fabric of the planet.

Without fungi breaking down cellulose and lignin, dead plants and trees would accumulate and in time there wouldn't be enough accessible carbon to maintain the CO_2 cycle, Elio Schaechter explains in *In the Company of Mushrooms*. Life on earth would cease without our fungal cohort.

Mycorrhizae are rootlike filaments you might find under any fallen log or rotting leaf in the soil. These networks of fungal strands help plants to absorb water, break down mineral compounds, and prevent erosion.

The basketball-sized giant puffball in my backyard had been fed by a miles-long network of underground threads, a symbiotic relationship with the surrounding living organisms. The puffball consumes some of the available energy, but also provides stability and benefit outweighing what it takes.

This is the nature of Justice in the tarot—balance.

In the court systems, Justice is often blindfolded to represent impartiality—detachment from emotion or favor. In the tarot, Justice stares straight at the querent, asking you to personally consider your actions and circumstances.

"The Fool is faced with consequence." writes Courtney Weber in *Tarot for One*. "Any imbalances the Fool created or received so far in the journey will be rectified—whether the Fool likes it or not."

Fungi tend to support balance and stability. According to Stamets, fungal networks of mycelium run through the forest soil, balancing resources and maintaining biodiversity.

He has conducted studies determining that mycelium networks pass nutrients from trees with resources to spare to struggling trees, perhaps seedlings growing in the shade, unable to produce enough food from photosynthesis. This transfer takes place between multiple species, ensuring the overall health of the forest. By promoting biodiversity, the fungi can promote their own survival.

"I believe fungi have evolved to support habitats over the long term, protecting generations hundreds of years into the future," writes Stamets. "Saprophytic mushrooms gobble up debris fallen from the trees and prevent invasion by parasites. The mycorrhizae channel nutrients, expand root zones and guard against parasites. Similarly, endophytic fungi chemically repel bacteria, insects and other fungi."

Stamets has studied and written extensively about mycoremediation—using fungi to repair the damage we've done to the environment. He's conducted experiments using oyster mushrooms to remediate oil spills. In a controlled experiment, diesel-contaminated soil samples treated with mycoremediation techniques had reduced petroleum hydrocarbons from 20,000 parts per million to 200 parts per million in eight weeks. He's studied the ability of some fungi to feed on the radioactive wastes in Chernobyl. The promise of this approach to repairing the landscape is incredible.

"The rule in nature, when a species exceeds the carrying capacity of its host environment, its food chains collapse, and diseases emerge to devastate the population of the threatening organism. I believe we can come into balance with nature using mycelium to regulate the flow of nutrients," Stamets writes.

And yet, the sword of Justice can cut both ways. We've unleashed inexorable fungal plagues through inadvertent actions.

Chestnut blight and Dutch elm disease have decimated the eastern deciduous forests. Butternut canker, beech bark disease, and white pine blister rust ravage much of the woods that are left.

White nose syndrome, a fungal pathogen introduced from Europe, has killed over 6 million bats—more than 90 percent of some populations in the upper Midwest. Chytrid fungus imported from Africa is killing our frogs and salamanders.

The damage wrought on our eastern woods by invasive fungal pathogens is incomprehensible. But it is the bargain we accepted for the convenience of our globalized economy.

But these disasters are just part of a much broader wave of environmental destruction and injustice.

The endless frontier of abundance our economy thrives on is a delusion—we are living through a temporary and tenuous gluttony. The bill will come due. Justice's scales will be balanced.

Justice warns us that we benefit from the exploitation of

the planet and the poor. Our economic, political structures are bent toward our continued comfort, based on a false promise of ever-increasing growth.

We cede our morality to absentee, short-time corporate overlords committed to the next quarter's profitability.

Reflecting on this card, I consider my footprint, my role in killing life on this planet, my choices. The impact of our actions will not be in some distant dystopian future, but rather something my sons will suffer in their lifetimes.

A slow greening of the industrialized economy will not save us. There won't be some great turn, a mass movement. It can't happen in time. There are barely any wholly intact ecosystems left on the planet. We're drawing down reserves to meet our daily demand for goods and energy. We promote subsidies that kill the planet.

"If psychosis is the attempt to live a lie, the epidemic of psychosis of our time is the life of believing we have no ethical obligation to our planetary home," writes Theodore Roszak in *Ecopsychology*. "In our hearts, we know there is something maniacal about the way we are abusing the planetary environment."

So where does that leave us? Do we withdraw into some off-the-grid shack and homeschool our kids? Do we ignore our reality?

Rachel Pollack writes that Justice's sword is an emblem of action. To learn about our role in the universe (IX, The Hermit) and develop the will to do what needs to be done (VIII, Strength), but to do nothing, renders our lives and efforts meaningless.

"We form our future selves by the actions we take now," Pollack writes. "Can we look honestly at ourselves and accept the truth of what we have done, what has happened to us, where the balance rests between our own actions and the circumstances of our lives?"

Nature has a profound capacity for healing and restoration.

"A single ten-inch giant puffball has as many as 7 trillion (7,000,000,000,000) spores. If each of those spores grew and yielded a ten-inch puffball, the combined puffball mass would be 800 times that of the earth," writes David Landers, a biology student at Cornell, on its mycology department blog.

No problem is too big. Maybe Stamets is right, that there is a way to use fungi to build resilient communities that care for each other and restore abundance.

Mushrooms and mycelium may be a tactic for repairing broken landscapes. But to achieve any lasting version of Justice for the planet, we need to address systemic societal injustice.

I think about Paul Hawken, who writes, "It is critical to realize that underlying the extermination of nature is the marginalization of human beings. If we are to save what is wild, what is irreparable and majestic in nature, then we will ironically have to turn to each other and take care of all human beings here on Earth. There is no boundary that will protect an environment from a suffering humanity."

Low-income and minority communities bear an unequal burden for our pollution. Who lives in proximity to our incinerators, toxic waste sites, and coal-fired power plants?

I think of the residents of Flint, Michigan, who haven't been able to drink their tap water since 2014.

I imagine the mycelium of the giant puffball reaching under my house, throughout the backyard and into the woods, supporting a community of living beings. I imagine a future where we will be like that network, grounded, rooted, complementary.

Outside in the backyard, I hold the giant puffball in both hands, showing my son.

There are more puffballs hidden in the leaves nearby. The biggest one must weigh half as much as my four-year old. We hug it to our bodies, and think about what it means for something like this to spring out of the ground unbidden.

We've made choices. The consequences that follow will be outside of our control.

XII

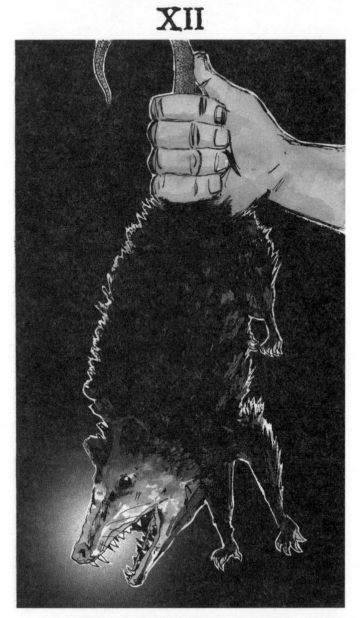

THE HANGED MAN

CHAPTER 12
THE LAST MARSUPIAL IN THE NORTHERN HEMISPHERE

A wonder of mammalian evolution lives under my crawlspace.

The Virginia opossum, part of a large and varied clade of marsupials, is much more closely related to Australian koala bears and kangaroos than the racoons and skunks it cohabitates with in my backyard.

Yet, the opossum is reviled.

We consider them lower than a dangerous or frightening creature. It is merely disgusting, some misshapen offspring of a slow-witted demon and a wharf rat

Its liquid black eyes are due to its huge pupils, an adaptation to its nocturnal existence—yet we see them as evidence of its soulless nature.

They seem to have too many teeth, and in fact they do, more teeth than any other mammal in North America.

We most often see them crushed on our highways, a bloody flattened scab or a bloated meat sack rotting on the berm.

You may see one stumbling slowly through your backyard and feel compelled to brain it with something.

Their general appearance calls to mind something sick or injured, near death. And by all accounts, they are.

They are hated, but thrive. The Virginia opossum, North America's only marsupial animal, doesn't get by on niceties.

It eats the dead. It fucks its kin. It spreads. A mostly unchanged version of this fanged dust mop has scraped and scuttled through the world since the age of dinosaurs.

The opossum is a fine stand-in for the Hanged Man. The original card depicts a man being punished by the masses. He is someone to ridicule. He refuses to conform.

He seems to have accepted his fate, for the look on his fate is almost beatific, smiling and serene. He has a halo in many versions.

And yet, his circumstance did not come without suffering. He is helpless and has no power to control the outcome.

To quote Thomas Hobbes, life can be "solitary, poor, nasty, brutish, and short." It is especially so for an opossum.

The female opossum gives birth just twelve days after mating. The mobile fetuses, not only blind, but without developed gastrointestinal tracts, lungs, or kidneys, climb from the birth canal to the mother's pouch.

For two months, the young are sealed to their mothers' teats, unable to open their mouths to detach from swollen nipples. At three months, the young are weaned. They have to find food.

Everything kills them – raptors, dogs, coyotes, red foxes, raccoons, bobcats, and even large snakes. They are slower than every animal that pursues them.

When confronted by a threat, young opossums can fall into a catatonic state—eyes glazed, tongue lolling, unflinching—feigning death.

Two thirds of them will be killed within their first month after weaning.

And yet somehow they persist.

The opossum is pushing its population boundary north faster than it can evolve. Despite being poorly adapted to the cold, solitary opossums will suffer through the winter.

Unprotected tails and ears will be frostbitten and torn. They'll subsist on roadkill, and shelter in place throughout the worst weather.

Toward the end of winter, opossum mating season begins. The species is highly tolerant of inbreeding. Mate selection seems to come down to male body mass.

The biggest, fattest male opossums mate with the most females.

In the Great Lakes area, the northern part of the opossum's range, females only have a single litter of offspring before dying. The lifespan in the wild is under two years. Captives may live three or four years. They are one of the shortest-lived mammals for their size.

About a million Virginia opossums are taken by trappers in the U.S. each year, despite a lack of interest. They just show up in the trap.

The going rate for the fur is less than three dollars per pelt.

Most of the juveniles are too small to be worth cleaning, and larger females' furs are usually damaged.

"When the little ones climb out of the female's pouch, she carries them around on her back—they're pulling out all her guard hairs," explains Vern Snyder, a wildlife technician with the Ohio Department of Natural Resources. "In the furrier trade, they call them mohawks. If you look at female opossums, they have guard hairs pulled out on either side with a stripe of long hair down the middle."

The big joke in the trapping community is that nothing is faster than an opossum.

"They're the first ones there. They'll ruin a coyote set for you," Snyder said. "If you set for raccoon or fox, you will catch opossums."

Snyder and his sons are trappers, and they caught three opossums as bycatch while trying for raccoon and fox over a late winter weekend.

Few trappers target them unless someone is asking for a nuisance removal, but Snyder said he takes a few each year as he feels its his role to keep down the predators of ground nesting birds.

There is a famous story about President Taft feasting on an eighteen-pound whole cooked possum and taters in Atlanta,

Georgia and I asked Snyder if he had ever tried it.

"Beaver and muskrat are pretty good eating… But opossum, I have to say no."

Despite being unwanted and incredibly adaptable, opossums are declining in Ohio.

According to twenty-eight years of roadkill survey data from ODNR, opossum populations have shrunk by over 40 percent since 1989 in Ohio. Both skunk and woodchuck populations experienced a similar decline over the same period in this study.

A survey of bowhunter observations from 1990 to present shows a similar decline in opossums.

Biologists do not know what is causing the decline. It seems unlikely that it is disease or environment, as opossums tend to benefit from urbanization (urban opossums are 34 percent larger than their rural counterparts due to access to pet food, trash, crops, and other human-generated food sources).

The declining abundance of middle-sized animals like skunks and opossums may be a corrective function with the return of an apex predator to the landscape.

Mesopredator Release is a biological theory that suggests humans' systemic eradication of apex predators (such as wolves) in the previous century had lead to population explosions of smaller predators, and also subsequent declines in prey species further down the food chain, like songbirds.

Now that coyotes are found in all eighty-eight Ohio counties, nature may be balancing the scales. If you overlay the coyote data from the bowhunter survey with the opossum data, they are inversely proportionate. Coyote populations have tripled over the same time period that opossum populations have been halved.

Coyotes are native to the American west and started migrating east of the Mississippi in the beginning of the last century. They grow to about fifty pounds and are found everywhere from the farm country to the busiest urban streets.

Raccoons, bigger and more equipped to fend off predatory pressures than opossums, are not suffering the same declines. In fact, their populations are growing. Studies show less than three percent of raccoons are killed by coyotes.

The opossum just doesn't have the same wherewithal. But it turns out we need them now.

If there is an animal people hate more than opossums, it's deer ticks. The bloodsucking bastards spread Lyme disease, a dangerous and painful condition that just arrived in Ohio.

In Ohio, Lyme disease reports are up 33 percent from 2016 to 2017. The host ticks are spreading across the state rapidly since 2009.

Black-legged deer ticks also cling to opossums. But they are constantly grooming themselves. The opossums eat the ticks, up to 5,000 in a year per animal. As the dimly aware opossum plods along chewing on parasites, it is protecting us as well.

They are immune to rabies and the bites of North American venomous snakes, and kill them with impunity.

They'll finish a maze with food in it faster than a rat or a cat. It will remember where the food is the next time it attempts the maze—with better cognition than dogs.

They don't have any power. They are ridiculed. They scavenge the roadsides, cleaning up after us.

Think about these things when you see one of these stumbling along in the dark street – what it has survived, and what it yet must do, before its short, brutish life is over.

XIII

DEATH

CHAPTER 13
WHO OWNS THE WHOLE RAINY, STONY EARTH?

They haunt us with black wings and thick rending beaks for carrying rotten flesh to the heavens. Our most potent symbol of death stalks us at every turn.

Crows flourish on our waste, and the denuding of the native landscape. They thrive in our wormy suburban lawns and carrion-smeared streets, supermarket dumpsters and restaurant spillage.

There are more wild crows today than at any point in the history of the planet.

Lyanda Lynn Haupt writes that the ratio of crows to humans has remained constant for the last several thousand years. As our populations balloon, the crows follow.

According to crow researcher John Marzluff, crows have been conjoined and coevolving with us since the late Pleistocene at least. They are eight times as abundant within one kilometer of people than they are at further distances. The mortality rate for adult crows living near humans over a two-year period is 2.3 percent, versus 38.9 percent mortality rate for crows living in unsettled landscapes.

We are linked.

There is no wild animal we are more likely to encounter, no creature we more closely resemble in our behaviors.

We are long-lived, vocally oriented, and reliant on memory. We care for those of our own species. Our young spend years living at home, learning how to become successful adults. We engage in foreplay, mate for life, cheat on our partners.

We congregate in large groups. We cooperate to drive away enemies. We mete out justice.

Crows and humans learn, socially transmitting knowledge to our kin and associates. This allows us to adapt through cultural evolution to keep pace with changes in our environments.

Corvids (crows, ravens, jays, and their ilk) are some of the most intelligent animals on the planet, on par with dolphins and primates. We often attach humanlike attributes and mental states to crows—anthropomorphizing what we imagine they are experiencing. They seem to enjoy play. They luxuriate in smearing formic acid on their bodies, an intoxicating substance they bleed from the bodies of ants. We perceive crows as being creative, vengeful, and bold.

And while humans and corvids have a similar brain-size to body-size ratio, bird brains are organized differently. Instead of a cerebral cortex, birds have developed something called the hyperstriatum.

"The larger the hyperstriatum, the better the birds fare on intelligence tests," writes Candace Savage in *Bird Brains*.

"Social animals must be natural psychologists to recognize and remember mates and companions, to discern and interpret subtle shadings in appearance and behavior," writes Savage. "The tone of a call, contour of the features, permit an individual to read the mood and intentions of its associates. It is the ability to seize meaningful details from a hubbub of meaningless activity."

Crows and humans are both dietary generalists, requiring a mental flexibility and memory to adapt to a wide range of potential food sources.

Are corvids conscious? Do they have ideas or see images in their heads? Can crows reason?

Animals have reflexive or pre-programmed responsive behaviors that have been refined and adapted through natural selection, reactions to stimuli in an environment.

Yet crows, in order to survive and even thrive in a rapidly changing human-shaped world, need plasticity and flexibility in their intelligence, to fill the gaps between programmed responses, and considered actions based on memory and learning.

One of the behaviors that sets crows apart from many other animals is the crow funeral.

Crows respond strongly to a dead member of their own species, gathering and pecking at the body, calling raucously.

What are they doing?

Kaeli Swift is a University of Washington PhD candidate studying crow death behaviors and trying to answer that question.

Are crows afraid of death? Do the crows understand that their dead companion is not coming back?

"Crows recognize an animal laid out on the ground is different from other individuals. They recognize the state of being not alive. But do they have a concept of death—that life is finite? We don't know."

But the crow is one of the few animals that has a specific reaction to the dead of its own species.

Swift has conducted studies in the Seattle area, trying to parse how crows react to a dead stuffed crow and predators introduced to their environments. The research suggests the purpose for the crow funerals is to learn about potential threats and to communicate those threats to the broader crow community with the loud calls.

What killed their fellow crow? And what happens next? The noisy crows are as curious and anxious as we are about our corporeal ends.

Crows also serve as a reminder of our own mortality. According to Haupt, crows are one of the only animals associated with death that many of us are likely to see. This is not a role most people appreciate.

In Ohio, there is basically no closed season for shooting

crows and no bag limit.

Haupt suggests instead of hating or fearing crows, we should consider their presence a reminder to live as if death were around each corner, fanatically, creatively, joyfully.

"We are all nearly dead," Haupt writes in *Crow Planet*. "In light of that, our relentless, frenzied, earth-killing over-outfitting of our temporal bodies may be misguided."

In the tarot tradition, the card Death signifies an ending—irrevocable and inevitable. Many readers avoid its literal meaning, focusing on the symbolic interpretations for endings and new beginnings.

But to avoid the literal meaning of the card feels antiseptic and naive.

It's as if we can't bear to look at it directly. We ignore death in the hope that it doesn't turn toward us. We try not to attract its attention.

Even just a few decades ago, death was a common experience in of our lives. My grandparents and great-grandparents died in their homes, not in hospitals. We held their bodies. We mourned.

But today the dying and the deceased are "swept under the rug," writes Sallie Nichols in *Jung and Tarot*. "We put death in strangers' hands, distance ourselves physically and psychologically. Our fear of death prevents us from contemplating it at all. Yet each day our physical bodies make giant strides to death's door."

In my dark hours, when I feel anxiety and dread, the only image of my own death I can find comforting is to be consumed by scavengers and other recycling organisms, to feel as if I am part of some bigger whole, that I can be useful in some way.

We are alienated from the life on this planet—the word means to make unfriendly, hostile, or indifferent especially where attachment formerly existed. I don't want to die looking at my cell phone on the toilet. I don't want to be buried in a sealed toxic capsule.

I want to be carried off to the sky by black wings. I want to sink into my home in the black earth.

The crows and death are an antidote against complacency and self-pity.

XIV

TEMPERANCE

CHAPTER 14
THE BITTERNS OF MENTOR MARSH

Temperance is a card of redemption.

In a traditional tarot deck, Temperance features a winged angel standing with one foot on land and one in the water. The angel pours a liquid from one vessel into another—suggesting measurement, combination.

Our current usage of the word temperance mostly refers to the avoidance of alcohol, but the tarot meaning is less rigid.

Temperance is not blind abstinence, but a careful and measured response to an unbalanced situation. It suggests a path to reconcile and overcome our destructive nature.

Temperance tells us a situation is not irreparable. But change will not come easy—it would require commitment.

Twenty-five miles east of downtown Cleveland, workers wage perpetual battle for the soul of one of Lake Erie's most important wetlands.

Mentor Marsh lies in a former channel of the Grand River, just west of Fairport Harbor.

It had once been a huge swamp forest, teeming with rare birds and turtles, and had provided habitat for spawning fish.

Then in the summer of 1966, the Osborne Concrete and Stone Co. dumped 265,000 tons of salt mining waste on a property near the marsh, poisoning a feeder tributary killing the wetland's native trees and plants.

Soon after the company poisoned the marsh, an invasive salt-loving reed grass swept in—*Phragmites australis.*

The European Common Reed grows fifteen feet tall and chokes out every living thing in its path. It grows to such heights and densities that it crowds out native species, creating a monoculture wasteland of biologically worthless vegetation.

You've seen stands of phragmites waving in the wind—a deceptively pleasing sea of green leaves and seed heads blowing in the wind over a scarred landscape. It has colonized roadside ditches and wetlands across the country.

But it offers no food, little shelter, and crowds out everything else.

Try to walk into a patch of phragmites and the reeds will block your path, cut your skin. The plants grow as dense as one stalk per every inch. The old stems are so tough, the stalks rot for three years before breaking back down into the soil.

Mentor Marsh is one of the biggest stands of invasive phragmites in Ohio. The 765-acre site was the state's first nature preserve, and it's managed by the Cleveland Museum of Natural History.

About a decade ago, Jim Bissell, the curator of botany and director of natural areas at the Cleveland Museum of Natural History had cleared a swath of reeds from the periphery of a popular boardwalk to protect it from frequent phragmites fires, which allowed birders a better view of species that might still visit the marsh. The following spring, native plants emerged from the seedbank.

The quick recovery gave the museum hope for restoring the marsh. They would try to clear the whole damn thing.

In subsequent years, the museum has secured grant funding to kill the phragmites with herbicide applications, cutting it down, chewing up the tough stalks with heavy machinery.

"We've taken the biggest stand of phragmites in the state of Ohio and put the smack-down on it," said David Kriska, biodiversity coordinator at the Cleveland Museum of Natural History. "Over 90 percent of it is dead and knocked down. It's going to rally from the roots—that's what it does. But we've really done a lot to knock it back.

"One of our goals is to turn the site from the biggest stands of phragmites, to the biggest stand of marsh milkweed. The marsh is right on the monarch butterfly's migratory corridor. It's a long-term goal."

After a few years of working on this huge project, the museum hired Ben Piazza to manage the remediation full time in the spring of 2017. Piazza had been killing invasive plants for most of a decade, but he'd never seen anything like Mentor Marsh before—hundreds of acres of solid phragmites.

"They'd been treating it for years, but the phragmites have decades of stored energy under the ground—tubes as big around as your wrist getting fatter and fatter," Piazza said. "With something like this you have to starve the rhizome. We've gotten to the tipping point now where it is on its way out. We're on the cusp of flipping it, but you don't know what's going to emerge next year until the plants start popping up in the spring."

In addition to killing the phragmites, the museum is accelerating the recovery by planting more than 19,000 plants in 2017. Kriska has documented sixty species of native plants reemerging at the site.

"We have nodding bur-marigold taking off where the phragmites have fallen down," Kriska said. "Spikerush is starting to cover the western central basin."

Rare birds such as Virginia, king, and sora rails, common gallinules and Wilson's snipe are now nesting at the site. And native fish such as northern pike and yellow perch are starting to use the marsh for spawning habitat and a nursery.

Two of the most secretive birds in the state are now using the recovered site—least bitterns and American bitterns.

The least bittern is listed as threatened in Ohio, and the American bittern is listed as endangered. They are quiet, deliberate herons that can stalk through the swamps without ever being noticed.

"Bitterns are all about secrecy and stealth," Kriska said. "I've seen them use phragmites for habitat, but only where it is patchy and thin. If it gets too dense, they aren't able to push through it. In the western basin, where the work is furthest along, you see the most bitterns. It's a mosaic patchwork of open water and vegetation, so they can skulk and pounce on prey."

The American bittern stands two and a half feet tall, with mottled tan and cream plumage. When it feels threatened, the bird stands perfectly still with its beak raised straight to the sky, blending perfectly into the dried vegetation surrounding it. During the mating season in the spring the males' territorial advertisement call sounds like a giant drop of water falling into a jug.

"The male's call is preceded by clacking and gulping. To accomplish the pump-er-lunk sound, the male inflates his esophagus by way of almost violent body contortions—opening and closing his bill as if lunging for flying insects—and then uses the stored air to unleash his call. Repeated up to ten times in succession, the call probably serves as both a territorial signal and an advertisement for mates," writes the Cornell Lab of Ornithology.

The bitterns embody the vision of Temperance—cautious, winged creatures with one foot on land, the other in the water.

Bitterns need large, high-quality wetlands to thrive, but over the course of Ohio's history, developers and landowners have systematically destroyed 90 percent of the wetlands. Bitterns are widely distributed, but there are very few left in Ohio.

A rehabilitated Mentor Marsh would provide a great opportunity to boost the dwindling bittern populations in the Great Lakes region.

Several pairs of least bitterns used the Mentor Marsh for breeding habitat in 2017. But a different kind of imbalance doomed these individuals. All of the nests were raided by raccoons.

"Raccoons are super-adaptable predators, and their numbers in Northeast Ohio have gone up 800 percent in the last twenty years," Kriska said. "Our goal isn't to eradicate them, but to get the population down to reasonable levels."

Kriska would like to reintroduce state-threatened spotted and Blanding's turtles to the marsh where they belong. But Kriska has to get the raccoon population under control first or they will devour all of them in a summer.

Wildlife management is not organic or easy—we broke off our connection to the landscape, and now struggle to manage the unintended consequences of our decisions.

The marsh's stewards will have to keep out the whitetail deer and Canada geese from over-browsing the new growth. The city of Mentor has culled over 1,000 deer from the site over the last three years.

They will have to spray herbicides on secondary invaders, like purple loosestrife, lesser celandine, and non-native cattails. They will battle back the canary grass and Japanese knotweed springing up at the margins of the restoration, threatening to take over again.

It is clumsy, tedious, and never ending. But this project is a victory, not a stalemate.

We are learning how to restore and sculpt the landscape, to take care of our homes as if our lives depended on it, to learn to heal the destruction we've wrought.

It is holy work, to make this marshland whole.

THE DEVIL

CHAPTER 15
DARKNESS VISIBLE

One warm night near the summer solstice, hundreds of fireflies flew out of the grass and twinkled, ghostly green flares in the darkening suburban understory.

I snuck my six-year-old son out of bed, clambering under a half moon in pajamas.

A few bats swooped overhead. Junebugs bumped clumsily against our screen door. We found moths flitting in the porch lights. We listened to the green frogs chortling in the slough behind the house.

The boy and I ran through the night to gather the first lightning bugs of the summer and put them in a container to watch overnight.

We didn't know at the time we'd captured *Photuris pennsylvanica*, a predacious trickster. The female of this species mimics the flash patterns of other firefly species. When potential suitors come to investigate, these females eat them.

This betrayal represents just one example of the sordid behaviors of our beloved fireflies. About which most of us know nothing.

Fireflies are not flies but beetles. They exist on every continent except Antarctica, and there are about 2,000 described species worldwide. There are 150 species in North America, and 43 species of fireflies in Ohio. About 30 of those Ohio species can flash.

All of these species follow the holometabolus lifecycle—egg, larva, pupa, and adult—transforming from one form into another.

Lynn Frierson Faust, author of the definitive field guide to fireflies, describes the process as "the astonishing miracle of complete and profound reorganization of the body from active grub-like predator, to flying, flashing sex machine."

During their larval form, fireflies live in the damp areas in your yard for one to two years—and look and act like something out of a nightmare. They hunt in packs, tackling prey twice their size.

"Most of us have had this magical firefly experience as a kid. But they're not what we think, not what they seem. I would hate to break a child's heart," says Valerie Fetzer, Rocky River Reservation's Nature Center manager and naturalist for Cleveland Metroparks. "The larvae are carnivores, eating worms, snails, and slugs. They stalk the slimy mollusk's trail. They inject a toxin through their mouths and digest prey alive."

Fetzer pulls out an eight-by-ten photo she'd printed of the jagged tail end of a firefly larva hanging out of the shell of a much larger snail it was eating.

It had climbed up inside the snail. Something about it made my stomach lurch.

One of my favorite lines by Annie Dillard in *A Pilgrim at Tinker Creek* is, "Fish gotta swim and birds gotta fly; insects, it seems, gotta do one horrible thing after another."

Fireflies seem like obvious targets for predators, slow and highly visible. But the flash is a warning of their foul-tasting and even poisonous nature.

Fireflies can poison would-be predators through reflex bleeding. "They ooze a toxic substance, and in some cases the substance has the ability to glue the attackers mouth shut," Fetzer says.

Which brings us back to *Photuris*, the predatory adult firefly.

The purpose of the firefly's glow is sexual communication. Each species has its own flash pattern, with varying color, length, number of flashes, interval of time between flashes, time of night, and flight pattern.

Fireflies combine an enzyme Luciferase with a substrate Luciferin to produce light. The word "luciferin" is based off the word Lucifer, Latin meaning light-bringing or morning star.

"There are more males out there than females," Fetzer explains. "The females sit and wait while the males fly around and flash. If the female likes what she sees, she lights her own light until they are able to find each other."

The *Photuris* females have a large repertoire of flashes, and can mimic different species' patterns. When a male comes to investigate, the *Photuris* "goes for the neck," writes Faust. They attack the male fireflies aggressively, and focus on devouring the males' defensive toxic chemicals to pass on protection to their larvae.

The female *Photuris* is a highly effective liar.

David Livingstone Smith writes, in the book *Why We Lie: The Evolutionary Roots of Deception and the Unconscious Mind*, "Nature is awash in deceit."

Lying in nature is everywhere if we view a "lie" as any form of behavior that functions to provide others with false information. "If a creature cannot get what it wants from others by exercising force, it must do so by using guile," writes Smith.

Consider the eastern hognose snake: it is harmless, but if it is cornered it flares its neck and strikes aggressively (with its mouth closed) to appear dangerous. If that doesn't work to drive its potential predator away, it fakes its death—writhing on the ground, flipping over on its back, and lolling its tongue from its open mouth. It even bleeds from its eyes and begins to smell of rot.

There are male insects that mimic females to steal mating offerings from other males. Less dominant male cuttlefish present as female to get close to potential female mates without being

103

pushed out by more dominant males.

Natural selection favors deception. It gives liars an advantage in the struggle to survive and mate.

Again, deception doesn't need to be verbal. It is any effort to provide false information—consider breast implants, hairpieces, phony smiles. Lies underpin all of evolution, even our own.

"Children are often told not to lie, but more frequently are taught to lie in a socially acceptable manner," writes Smith. "Feign respect for others, write thank you notes for disappointing gifts, refrain from telling grandma her breath stinks. Socially appropriate lying isn't tolerated, but mandated. A child that doesn't master this faces disapproval and ostracization."

The Devil is known as the Father of Lies.

In the tarot tradition, the Devil is depicted as a humanoid chimera—a handsome human shape with a goat's legs and horns, bat wings and dragon's tail. He is a tempter, a sadistic dungeon master, a gambler.

The Devil would encourage you to indulge in selfish pleasures.

He is often pictured with captives, a male and female in his thrall. The card is associated with addictions, self-destructive behavior, bad relationships. In *Mystical Origins of the Tarot*, Paul Huson interprets the card to represent "avoidable evil."

Like the female *Photuris* firefly, the devil doesn't chase his prey, but rather calls to our base instincts.

"In order to be caught [by The Devil], we must of necessity, take at least one innocent step forward," writes Sallie Nichols in *Jung and Tarot*.

The Devil is a way of personifying our own base urges that lead us astray. That's why the traditional cards picture both the deceiver and the deceived.

The Devil is our way of reconciling a world full of suffering. The Devil is a projection of our existential frustration with a distracted, or distant God. We created a scapegoat to soothe our psyches when the innocent suffer and the wicked flourish.

The *Photuris* firefly is a tempter and an effective predator. But it is not evil. Its behaviors are driven by the same motivations of all living things.

All biological life is driven by killing and eating itself – cows eating grass, people eating cows, crows eating people, mushrooms and fungi digesting dead organic matter.

It's all a big cosmic potluck. Every bite of food, every scrap of shelter, every molecule of fossil fuel, is built off the remains of something once alive.

But the bottom is falling out.

Firefly freaks (and insect enthusiasts in general) have been concerned about a hunch that insect populations have been crashing for years. But a study published in 2017 puts a sharp point on the issue, outlining a dire and specific case study in Europe that points to pending ecosystem collapse.

Researchers, over the course of twenty-seven years in sixty-three protected nature reserves in Germany, estimated about an 80 percent decline in flying insect biomass over nearly three decades of study.

The rapid decline of insect populations, while in itself depressing, will have cascading effects on the animals that insects support in the ecosystem. Bird, bat, and amphibian populations are already declining significantly worldwide. Without pollinators, most plant species we depend on for food will no longer be able to function–impacting our food sources, as well as every other creature in an ecosystem.

I don't think serious researchers even dare extrapolate what a world without insects would look like. But it's hard to imagine how our ecosystems still function at all with only 20 percent of the bugs that should be on the planet still flying around.

Fireflies face several specific challenges. We are paving over fields and forests where they live. We spray our sprawling lawns with pesticides. Flood lights beam from every new house, disrupting firefly mating and communication. Catching fireflies is one of my most vivid and magical childhood memories, and I loved chasing them with my son. I would have let him keep them overnight in his room. But today there are too many pressures on these insects.

After a short visit, we take our fragile captives outside and let them go at the edge of the dark woods.

XVI

THE TOWER

CHAPTER 16
BIRDS RAIN DOWN FROM THE SKY

My first introduction to Tim Jasinski, a wildlife rehabilitator at the Lake Erie Nature & Science Center, was a few winters ago. I had been out scanning for rare seabirds along the mouth of the Cuyahoga River with two naturalists, and we'd stumbled onto an injured herring gull.

It was limping around, bleeding, unable to fly. I wouldn't have given the gull a second thought. The bird was as good as dead, and would be recycled back into the nutrient chain in one way or another.

To my disbelief, the naturalists cornered the bird, slipped a hat over its eyes to calm it down, and wrapped it in a coat.

They kept the gull calm and comfortable, waiting for Jasinski to pick it up and nurse it back to health.

This wasn't a rarity, but rather one of the most common species, a Wal-Mart parking lot bird. It had dirty gray feathers, and a look in its eye that suggested it would bite your kid and steal his French fries.

Jasinski was about to drive halfway across Cleveland to show this bird more compassion than I'd consider possible.

I didn't meet Jasinski that day. I ran back home to escape the frigid wind off the lake. But I was stunned that someone could break through the barrier seemingly separating the worlds of people and wildlife.

So much of my energy over the past several years had been spent handwringing about the environment in the abstract: writing articles, donating to nonprofits, protesting pipelines.

I hadn't realized someone could just reach out with their hands to help.

That is the nature of the Tower—one minute you are snug in some structure that you've built to avoid the chaos of life, the next you are flying out of a window and your whole damn worldview has been exploded.

I heard about Jasinski again in the fall of 2016. Birders had stumbled onto eighteen woodcocks in downtown Cleveland. These shy, migratory shorebirds had gotten lost in the city. I had actually seen one on Euclid Avenue, scurrying along the sidewalk in the shadows of the buildings.

I remembered thinking, "Cool—a woodcock," and kept on walking. I read on the birding message boards that Jasinski had set out to rescue as many as he could.

But a bigger effort would be required to gather information and prevent more needless deaths.

The following spring, before the annual bird migration started, Jasinski joined a partnership with the Cleveland Museum of Natural History, the Lake Erie Science & Nature Center, Cleveland Metroparks, and the Akron Zoo to form "Lights Out Cleveland," part of a statewide program to try to limit and learn from city-centric bird deaths during the annual migration periods.

Traveling between the tropics and the arctic is dangerous and difficult. Songbirds face an 85 percent annual mortality rate during migration, according to the U.S. Forest Service. And humans are making things harder.

The U.S. Forest Service estimates about a billion birds are killed annually from anthropogenic (i.e. human-based) causes in the United States. And at least 100 million birds die annually from building strikes alone.

Each spring and fall, millions of songbirds fly over us through the night. "As you sleep, a thousand orioles might travel through a slice of sky above your bed, northward bound after a winter in Mexico," writes Miyoko Chu in *Songbird Journeys*.

The southern shore of Lake Erie is a critical stopover area for an avian migration that spans two continents. But our shining city on the lake presents two serious problems for the birds: excessive lighting and reflective glass.

"Birds use the stars to orient at night during migration," explains Andy Jones, curator of ornithology at the Cleveland Museum of Natural History. "When birds encounter an area with a low cloud ceiling they can't see the stars. If a few buildings are brightly lit, they reorient toward the building."

One of the most dramatic examples of this occurred in 2015 at the September 11 Memorial at the World Trade Center during the museum's tribute light display, when more than 15,000 birds swarmed in the cones of light cast by the memorial. In videos of the event, they look like dust motes swirling in the massive beams. Birds started falling out of the sky in exhaustion.

And then there's glass.

"Birds have evolved for millions of years without glass in the environment," Jones said. "Every one of us has walked into a sliding glass door. If you're a bird, you might only get to make that mistake once. With young birds—which make up much of the fall migration—their skulls haven't totally calcified. A building strike is more likely to kill them than an adult."

In a study conducted at Cleveland State University Campus, Jones found more bird deaths occurring at building facades with higher percentages of glass, and the presence of trees within five meters of a window also increased the mortality.

The site of the 2018 Super Bowl, U.S. Bank Stadium in Minneapolis, is a high-profile contributor to bird mortality for this reason. Ornithologists warned the glassy building reflecting open sky and tree branches would be a notorious bird killer along the Mississippi Flyway—and it is.

Minnesota Audubon has estimated that the stadium kills twice as many birds as any other building in the Twin Cities region.

The Javits Center in New York City had a similar reputation, until it applied imprinted patterns of white dots on its glass panels and cut the bird deaths by 90 percent in 2014.

There are ways to address the problem if we are willing to fix it.

In March 2017, Jasinski took to the streets with a small group to help recover the wounded, and catalog the dead, to try to gather data on what structures were killing our migratory birds.

Jasinski and Jones are developing a database to try to answer questions like: What direction are most of the injured birds coming from? Which buildings or areas are the big attractors? Does distance from Lake Erie matter?

The project started with the spring migration, but really ramped up in the fall. Between June and September, the North American bird population basically doubles with a new crop of young of the year.

In the fall of 2017, Jasinski's team recovered 1,800 birds. About 1,200 of them wound up in the museum's freezer for specimens and study. But a third of the birds were released.

That number is significant achievement, Jones said, because Jasinski's release rate is much better than the average Lights Out program's survival ratio of one-to-four in other cities.

"A lot of the birds are stunned and just need a few hours to be released. Tim has learned how to get to them quickly, and keep them dark and comfortable," Jones said.

The big reason for the higher rate of recovery compared to other programs is that Jasinski prioritizes birds that are alive before anything else.

"Knowing how to handle injured and sick birds is a delicate process," Jasinski explained. "Our team has a specific set of guidelines. Any live bird goes in a paper bag. We close it with paper clip and get the bird to a car as soon as possible to de-stress. A lot of organizations carry the birds around in their bags the whole morning. We get them away from the noise of people talking, wind blowing, and traffic. As soon as we get back to the Nature Center, we get them medication right away and put the birds in an enclosure where they can feed. Most start feeding instantly."

The Plain Dealer featured Jasinski's efforts in September 2017 and the article included a gallery of photos. You see Jasinski holding a yellow-breasted chat – a bird most of us have never seen – with its highlighter yellow breast and dark eyes, ringed in white.

In another photo, a Wilson's warbler peeks its tiny head and beak between Jasinski's fingers to sip medicine from a plastic syringe.

Jasinski's team recovered twenty-five species of warblers in the fall of 2017, in addition to other rarities like sora rails, yellow-bellied sapsuckers, vireos, kinglets, and flickers.

But if you ask Jasinski to recall his favorite experience so far, it's a grasshopper sparrow—a brown little prairie bird, native to the open grasslands of the eastern and central U.S. Its populations have been declining by 8.4 percent per year in Ohio since 1966. Overall the population has experienced a cumulative decline of 75 percent since the 1960s.

You might never know if it were gone. Most of us never knew it at all.

"It was puffed up on the sidewalk next to a window, people walking right by without noticing," Jasinski said. "I netted it, and it was badly spinning in circles. I didn't think it would survive. But we got the bird on heat and medications right away, and every day it got better."

The bird strikes echo the meaning and imagery of the Tower.

In most decks, the card shows a man and woman thrown from a tall building, struck down by God. The most common interpretation of its meaning is upheaval, a shocking incident or information that radically changes your understanding.

The event seems violent, like a punishment. But writer Rachel Pollack explains that it can be a breakthrough, a warning. "The Tower shows us a moment where we see the truth—and that experience can be shattering."

Between 1967 and 2017, the population of our common birds in the U.S. have declined by 70 percent, from 17.6 million to 5.35 million individuals according to Audubon.

Our children and grandchildren may never see the birds we grew up with. As Paul Huson writes, the Tower shows us, "What seems stable is not."

XVII

THE STAR

CHAPTER 17
THAW AND RETURN

On the first warm night of the year, still late winter, I held two of my sons' hands as we crept down the wet dark road leading through Cleveland Metroparks Brecksville Reservation.

We wore headlamps and walked slowly with a loose group of other guests—eyes trained to our feet to avoid stepping on any of the squirming creatures that had dragged themselves out of the barely unfrozen ground to find a mate.

My oldest son was seven years old and had the best night vision. He spotted the first one right away, a Jefferson salamander crossing the yellow painted lines of the middle of the road.

We surrounded the salamander in the light of our headlamps. It was about five inches long and slate gray, with bright blue flecks along its back. It had liquid black eyes, and a friendly looking face.

Of all of the amphibians in our region, the Jefferson salamanders are the first to emerge, sometimes as early as February in a mild winter.

At the first signs of thaw, Jefferson salamanders creep out of their hiding places and flock toward temporary woodland pools, traveling up to half a mile and even crossing snow and ice.

Jeffersons belong to the mole salamander family—*abystoma*. They spend nearly their entire lives underground in animal burrows, under logs, secreted along the roots of deciduous trees.

We soon found spotted salamanders, a closely related species that shares the same habitats and follows a similar life history. They are big plump salamanders, almost lewdly ribbed, decorated with stunning yellow spots.

Early spring is the only opportunity of the year to see them, as they will soon disappear back into their subterranean lairs.

We spent the night with these animals before they would disappear again, and participated briefly in their march toward the vernal pools.

Vernal pools are seasonal wetlands—small depressions in the woods where water collects temporarily and then evaporates after several months.

Harvard Forest aquatic ecologist Dr. Elizabeth Colburn, author of *Vernal Pools: Natural History and Conservation*, describes them as "Magical flooded woodland hollows."

In the late winter, tiny isolated pools across the Northeast and Upper Midwest fill up with snow melt, rain, and floodwaters. They transform from damp low spots in the woods, into clear pools seething with activity, and then slowly transform again into shallow mudholes in the late summer.

"The burgeoning life in tiny pools across the landscape carries a message of renewal and hope," writes Colburn. "It is an annual miracle."

Most of the pools were created at the melting of the last ice age. Continental ice sheets thawed and receded northward 10,000 years ago, leaving behind chunks of ice that settled into kettles in some places, scouring out depressions in the bedrock in other instances. The pools can also be created by a river gouging out a spot during a flood and then receding.

One of the essential requirements for a vernal pool is isolation. They can't be connected to any continuous surface water source. Any permanent, connected water source would support fish, large amphibians like bullfrogs, and other predators that would destroy the eggs and young of the amphibians that rely on these complex, delicate habitats.

The base of the food web in a vernal pool is fallen leaves.

Microscopic organisms decompose the debris, releasing nutrients that support the growth of algae. The algae feed dozens of species of microfauna and also have a symbiotic relationship with the salamander eggs, providing oxygen to the developing embryos in exchange for nutrients and carbon dioxide emitted by the developing eggs.

"This alga provides additional oxygen for the developing larvae and elevates their growth rate," explains Dr. Tim Matson, curator of vertebrate zoology at the Cleveland Museum of Natural History. "The alga's oxygen boost may allow the salamander larvae to attain a larger size and undergo metamorphosis a little sooner, which in dry years may mean the difference between survival and dying in a dried-up pool."

The eggs hatch in about thirty days and the larvae feed on tiny ostracods, crustaceans, and insects. The pools teem with caddisflies, mosquito larvae, midges, snails, leeches, shrimp, and flatworms.

When the pools dry up in the summer, invertebrates form desiccation-resistant cocoons and cysts, and utilize other strategies to survive the summer and reemerge in the spring. But the amphibians need to learn to find or dig a burrow, to hunt on land, and to stay below the frost line as winter sets in. Three years later, salamanders emerge from underground as sexually mature adults and make their way back to the spring pools where they were hatched.

The spotted and Jefferson salamanders often overlap in vernal pools with wood frogs.

These frogs are about two inches long with tan bodies and dark robber's masks. They are common across Northeast Ohio, and their range extends from the Appalachians to Alaska.

They emerge from the forest floor, frozen solid under the leaves, not breathing or eating. No heartbeat. No brain activity. They are functionally dead for months.

Laboratory studies have shown that wood frogs can survive the freezing of up to 70 percent of their body water, and uninterrupted freezing periods of over four weeks.

The wood frogs produce a natural antifreeze before going into hibernation, increasing glucose levels 60 times higher than normal.

"This allows the wood frogs to freeze, without internal cells freezing," Matson explained. "When animals freeze, the thing that kills them is ice crystals puncturing the cell membranes. Fluids leak out and the animal dies."

The cold can kill them if the freeze comes on too quickly, or if it goes too long.

"In a really cold winter without snow cover, a heavy penetrating frost goes deep and wood frogs can be exposed for so long they can't recover. But in a normal winter a high percentage of them survive," Matson explained. "Some frogs and toads don't have freeze tolerance, and have to burrow below the frost level. If they get caught in the freeze, they're dead. Green frogs and bull frogs can't stand freezing either. They will go into a ponds or lake and just lay on the bottom. But wood frogs have been found buried, rock hard just below the leaf litter. How can anything survive that?"

Miami University posted a six-minute time lapse video to YouTube of a wood frog thawing from a solid freeze. As ice melts off its skin, the tissues begin to twitch. The frog blinks its eyes three hours into the thaw. At four hours, it starts to breathe again. The limbs begin to spasm at six hours. After ten hours, the frog appears normal.

Each spring they rear up from the dead and drag their pale soft bellies to the pools to mate.

The males will arrive in droves and start calling. The call sounds like a bunch of drunken ducks, an overlapping quacking chorus.

They lie in wait for females to enter.

When a female jumps into the pool, the nearest male wraps his arms around her, locking thumbs together under her neck, and rides her down into the depths of the pool. He will not let go until she releases her eggs.

A drowned female wood frog in a pool could have dozens of males clinging to her limbs.

Multiple wood frog females will lay eggs in the same location within a pool, clustering together for warmth.

The tadpoles will begin life eating algae and leaves for two to four months while the pool shrinks, until it starts to get crowded and the tadpoles turn on each other. The strong eat the weak and the doomed, cannibalizing their siblings.

Author Donald Culross Peattie describes the breeding and rearing process as "a phlegmatic and persisting clasping, nothing more," in *An Almanac for Moderns*.

"It speaks of the return of life, animal life, to the earth. It tells of all that is most unutterable in evolution – the terrible continuity and fluidity of protoplasm, the irrepressible forces of reproduction—not mystical human love, but the cold batrachian jelly by which we vertebrates are linked to the things that creep and writhe and are blind, yet breed and have being."

But the poet Pattiann Rogers takes a more joyful view of the willful desire of life.

> *Who wouldn't sing—anticipating the belly pressed hard*
> *Against a female's spine in the steady rain*
> *Below writhing skies, the safe moist jelly effluence*
> *Of a final exaltation?*

The phenomena of amphibians migrating to the ephemeral pools where they were born echoes the themes of the Star.

The image most often used for this card features a woman

pouring water onto the earth in the middle of the night under a starry sky. In many examples, she is naked – exposed to the elements. It looks like a scene from a dream.

Many tarot writers associate the card with Persephone. In Greek myth, Persephone is the daughter of Demeter, captured by Hades, and taken to the underworld to be his queen. The gods intercede on her behalf and return Persephone to the earth. But for three months she must live in the land of the dead, and all of nature goes cold and dark until she returns.

In the tarot tradition, the card represents renewal after a difficult time. In Huson's *Mystical Origins of the Tarot*, the suggested interpretations are "Birth of hope. Healing."

The timing of the earliest amphibians returning to the vernal pools matches up with the Gaelic (and neopagan) festival of Imbolc in early February, associated with birth, cleansing, and lambing that takes place halfway between the winter solstice and the spring equinox.

Celebrate the end of a cold, long, dark winter with your own ode to the Star by walking dreamlike, quiet roads on a wet night with a headlamp, watching the amphibians return from the dead to replenish the forest pools.

XVIII

THE MOON

CHAPTER 18
THAT WHAT YOU FEAR THE MOST COULD MEET YOU HALFWAY

The moon loomed behind my house—huge and swollen, leering, larger than any full moon in decades—about a week after Donald Trump had been elected president.

It stared down from its nearest orbit in sixty-eight years, 14 percent closer to Earth than at apogee, its furthest orbit from our planet.

I could read by the moonlight, and it cast shadows of my hand hovering above my journal.

I wondered what goes on in the woods and fields on a night like this.

There was no wind, no clouds, barely a breeze. There was an odd stillness on the land. This time of year, animals are usually more noticeable—with trees stripped bare and dry leaves telegraphing every twitch in the forest. But this bright moonlight suppressed animal activity.

Most mammals are nocturnal or at least can function at night—it's one of the hallmarks of mammalian evolution. But during a bright full moon, many mammals and other creatures lay low.

Even mesopredators like opossums and skunks are scarce – as these are vulnerable to large owls and other apex predators.

"Fear of predation can impact population and community dynamics to a greater extent than predation itself," write biologists Laura Prugh and Christopher Golden in a study from the *Journal of Animal Ecology*.

The fear of being caught out in the open keeps things quiet.

The full moon inspires fear.

"On moonlit nights, figures skulk, glowing eyes peer from bushes and crazy laughter echoes; often boundaries of love and death, madness and sex get confounded, "writes Bernd Brunner in *Moon: A Brief History.* "

Current theories suggest the moon formed around 4.5 billion years ago when planets collided. A planet called Theia, about the size of Mars, crashed into the proto-earth called Gaia.

The impact pulverized Theia, and most of its material was absorbed by Gaia and formed Earth. The remaining debris was flung out into space and formed a cloud of debris around the planet which eventually formed into our moon.

The dark stains on the surface of the moon are called the lunar maria. Once thought to be seas, the dark splotches are basalt plains leftover from volcanic activity that took place around the time the moon formed. While earth's surface is constantly eroding or pushing up from tectonic activity, scientists estimate 99 percent of the moon's surface area is over three billion years old.

With no atmosphere, the moon is bombarded with cosmic debris. A football-sized meteorite crashes into the moon's surface every day; there are three trillion craters on the moon larger than one meter across.

It is a lifeless, airless, soundless hunk of rock. It is losing energy, slowing down, receding from us at a pace of 1.5 inches per year—about the same pace as human fingernail growth.

It stares down at us with the same side facing us each night —always hiding its backside. The moon rotates in sync with our planet, a phenomenon called tidal locking, so that 44 percent of its surface is always blocked from view.

This secretive moon is the gloomy wreckage of a long-dead planet, pummeled by fragments of space debris.

It is little wonder the moon expresses a mixed character in the tarot tradition.

Rachel Pollack writes that perception of the Moon card has changed, from primarily negative in the medieval interpretations (lunacy, danger, fear) to something more positive (calmness, mystery, and the wellspring of imagination) as our culture has evolved.

The consensus view is that the Moon tarot card signifies increased creative activity. But the wellspring of our creativity – the unconscious—is often a chaotic place. The word lunacy refers to intermittent periods of insanity purportedly driven by the cycles of the moon.

The moon follows a rise and fall pattern like the sun – rising in the east and setting in the west. People have used the lunar cycles and the location of moonrise and moonset for thousands of years to divide and structure time.

From my back porch, I looked up from my notebook and was surprised by how far the moon had moved across the sky in such a short time. I marked its passage through the trees.

I wondered about owls—if there may be one in my backyard waiting for some rodent to make a mistake.

The owl hunts by the light of the moon.

They have huge eyes compared to their body size, and they are designed for low-light. But an owl only has two or three times better night vision than the average human.

Wayne Lynch writes in *Owls of the United States and Canada*, "An open meadow in Virginia under clear skies and a full moon is roughly a million times brighter than inside a nearby leafy hardwood forest on a cloudy moonless night."

The owls can also rely on their hearing to find prey. The ears are asymmetrical—positioned offset in their skulls to help them better pinpoint the location of a sound. When you see an owl tilt its head, it is trying to figure out where a noise is coming from.

The fly slowly and silently with specially evolved wings and feathers that keep them aloft and dampen the sound of their flight.

Many cultures considered the owl a messenger of tragedy

and destruction.

Lynch writes that the Aztecs believed the owl was a symbol of the underworld. The Roman statesman Pliny the Elder wrote that the owl is a monster of the night, a harbinger of evil. The death of Julius Caesar was said to have been foretold by an owl.

And yet, much like interpretations of the Moon tarot—the owl has undergone a transformation. We are obsessed with owls. Fear has given way to something like reverence.

The moon and the owl stir up strong emotions. We surround ourselves with their representations. We project our undefined fears, distorted perceptions, our hopes on them.

They fascinate and call to us.

Just a year before, in November 2015, I'd ridden a ferry across a four-mile stretch of Lake Erie to Kelleys Island to learn about the lives of a secretive, migratory owl species.

The northern saw-whet owl is the most common owl in our area throughout the winter, though most people have never seen one.

These owls are tiny—about six inches tall. They're the smallest owl species in the eastern U.S. The owls are named after their call – *saw-whet* – a sound like a sharpening file dragged across the teeth of a saw blade.

Ornithologists assumed that northern saw-whet owls were permanent residents in the far north and rare in the U.S. even just a few decades ago.

The owls go unnoticed. They travel at night, barely make a sound during the non-mating season, and are near impossible to find during the day.

"Nobody even knew they were migratory until people noticed flocks of owls flying over the Great Lakes in the early twentieth century," says Scott Weidensaul, author and a leading researcher on Northern saw-whet owls.

Scientists are working with volunteers to track birds and try to better understand their movements.

I had joined Tom Bartlett, a retired biology teacher and research associate with the Cleveland Museum of Natural History, who has operated a saw-whet owl banding project for over a decade at Kelleys Island.

The banding is open to the public and a half-dozen people wearing headlamps had shown up by 7 p.m. Bartlett had strung a series of mist nets that looked like very fine volleyball nets throughout the woods, strategically placed to capture curious owls attracted by a recorded call.

Over 800 acres or approximately one-third of Kelleys Island is protected in its natural state. Of this, the Cleveland Museum of Natural History stewards 196 acres, or 25 percent of the preserve land on the island. The twenty-eight-acre Scheele Preserve on the northeast corner of the island protects a rare alvar forest habitat of hackberry, juniper, and rough-leaf dogwood trees.

Bartlett had caught the first owl around 8 p.m. We surrounded the nets with our collective headlamps as he disentangled the trapped little raptor. He pulled the fine mesh out of the owl's talons and sharp beak.

The owl's face was shaped like a sideways eight, two big liquid eyes with yellow irises and black pupils, surrounded by a fringe of whitish feathers sweeping back toward a darker brown-and-gray body. The owl had long black eyelashes and a sharp dark beak hooked down from the middle of the face.

Even with over 120 banding stations in the U.S. and Canada, and nearly half a million owls banded to date, researchers are just beginning to unravel the northern saw-whet owls' life history.

We looked on quietly in the presence of this little owl, held close. Bartlett closed a small numbered metal band around the bird's leg as his wife carefully noted the number of the band, time of day, the color of the owl's eyes, its sex, and its approximate age.

Bartlett finalized the documentation, and we surrounded him as he let the owl fly silently from his hands into the sky.

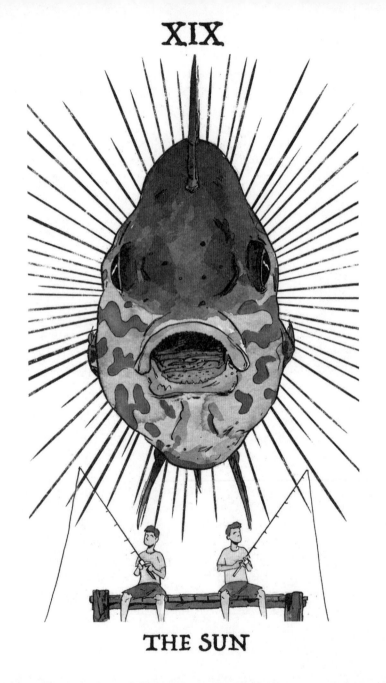

CHAPTER 19
THE SUNFISH

For most of my life, warm sun and bluegills have been conjoined.

My brother and I grew up fishing the Portage Lakes, a string of man-made reservoirs and glacial kettle lakes south of Akron, where the Cuyahoga dips down to meet the Tuscarawas River.

In my earliest memories, he and I are hoisting bluegills off their spawning beds with cane poles on my aunt's dock, piling up chunky panfish in an old wire fishing basket to show off to the adults later. I can still smell the sun baking the freshly stained dock, the boat exhaust, and the slime coat of the fish.

A school of large bluegills had pockmarked the lake bottom near the shore, digging out shallow circular depressions to host the next generation of panfish, each bluegill guarding its clearing from intruders.

We'd bait a long-shanked Eagle Claw hook with a waxworm, the plump translucent grub of a wax moth. We'd drop it off the side of the dock and into one of the circular nests for just a moment before the rod would shudder in our hands, the bobber pulled under, and we'd have another one.

Bluegills will eat anything they can fit in their mouths, from algae to insects, to smaller fish. In the summer months, they'd consume 35 percent of their body weight in food each week.

They are native to most of the eastern U.S. and Great Lakes region, but basically live in every lake, pond, or backwater in the U.S. due to stocking. They're members of the sunfish family, which includes the largemouth and smallmouth bass, crappie, and other panfish.

We didn't normally eat them. Nobody in our household wanted to help us filet and fry bluegill.

But lots of other folks did, and the state fisheries managers encouraged it. The thinking was that overpopulation of bluegills stunted the growth—too many mouths to feed led to smaller individuals.

Turns out decades of fisheries management was wrong.

Even today, there is no limit on bluegill in the Ohio state fishing regulations. You can keep as many as you want. But fish are getting smaller, everywhere, because of how we exploit their spawning regiment.

Bluegills build nests in the spring in colonies once the water temperature hits fifty-five degrees. Males use their tails to brush out those circular depressions a few inches deep and about a foot in diameter. They cluster together, males creating hundreds of these circular nests just a couple inches apart.

The biggest, most dominant males will take the positions in the center of the colony, the safest place to raise offspring and avoid predation from outsiders.

Males will circle and grunt in their nests to try to attract mates. The females will come into the colony to deposit eggs. Once a female has laid her eggs, the male fertilizes them and pushes her out of the nesting area.

A male will fan the eggs with its pectoral fins to keep them oxygenated and prevent them from being covered in silt. He will stand guard over the young—bluegill eggs would not survive without the male's protection.

The eggs will hatch in two to five days depending on the water temperature (warmer eggs hatch and grow faster), and the young will hide in the bottom of the nest. Dad will guard the juveniles for an additional week or more.

Bluegills that mature into parental males delay sexual

maturation and grow huge to build a nest and defend a brood. The process could take up to seven years to grow to a size to be a dominant panfish.

A huge male bluegill is a gorgeous animal—with a big fat forehead, a deep slab-shaped body with olive and purplish iridescent stripes, a prominent orange breast, turquoise blue jawline, and a black ear flap.

When they are young, bluegills are prey for all kinds of fish like largemouth bass. But once they get to be a certain size, they're too fast, their bodies are deep, and their fins are too spiny to be prey for anything but the biggest apex predators. The Ohio state record bluegill was 3.28 pounds and measured almost thirteen inches.

In the late spring you can see these big brutes chasing away intruders, flaring their gills in shallow water. These are the parental males. But there are other males lurking around.

The two mating strategies are labeled by fisheries biologists: cuckoldry and parental care.

In evolutionary biology, the term cuckold refers to male animals who are unwittingly investing parental effort in offspring that are not genetically their own.

They cuckolders "steal" fertilizations from the parental males that are investing resources and effort into care of offspring in two ways. Tiny sneaker males dare to sneak into nests when the big males aren't looking.

Sneaker male bluegill become sexually mature at age two. Unlike their beefy brethren, cuckold bluegills are tiny – but their gonads are huge. Looking at a photo of dissected cuckolder male bluegills, they might only measure two inches long, but their gonads take up the bulk of their body cavity.

In addition to sneaker males—tiny guys with big gonads, some males take a different approach. Slightly larger fish, aged four to five years, mimic female appearance and behavior to get access to nests which they surreptitiously fertilize.

Researchers have shown that these behaviors are not phases of all bluegill life histories—cuckolder males do not mature into parental males. Parental males do not grow up as sneakers.

The early mating males often die much younger than seven-year-old parental fish. While cuckolds make up 80 percent of the population of spawning male bluegill, their genes only account for 14 percent of the fertilization of the eggs.

So big adult males are key to survival. And yet, they're the ones we most often catch and keep. Intense spring fishing pressure removes the biggest fish and the only parental caretakers from the environment.

I think about the huge investment to become a parental male bluegill when my sons and I fish off my aunt's dock, decades later.

A giant 200-year-old oak tree had fallen into the lake during a recent storm, creating a hazard for navigation. But the fish love it.

My oldest son casts a bobber to the submerged trunk, and it is pulled under the moment it hits the water.

He pulls in the fish and I watch as he tentatively tries to grab it. Bluegills have ctenoid scales which are rough to the touch, and painful spines along the front of their dorsal fins. But once he has it secured in his grip, I watch him deftly remove his hook and throw his catch back in the lake.

My four year old struggles with the fish dangling off his rod, afraid and giddy.

They are tan and laughing.

All around the lake, cottages are busy with people. Pontoon boats run up and down the water. Mallards paddle by, looking to see if anyone has a handout. The Purple Martins – big glossy swallows—have returned from South America to nest in the bird houses above the dock.

In a lot of ways, not much has changed. There's a constancy

to this place, and to bluegill themselves. They've seemingly always been there. They're everyone's first fish.

In his essay "Bluegills and Rednecks," fly fishing author John Geirach writes, "Your old sweet spot doesn't care if you fish it any more or not. In fact, given the choice, it would probably just as soon you didn't."

But sitting in the sun with my boys, reeling in bluegill feels like a rite of passage, my old sweet spot seems welcoming.

Bluegills are part of my family's first meaningful connections with the natural world. We seek and hold wild quarry. I have photos of my brother and I posing with bluegills before we could talk. I have taken photos of my sons in the first weeks of their lives, posed with bluegills I've caught.

But the relationships with wild creatures are fraught. We learn about our capacity for inflicting pain—the act of skewering a live animal and the difficulty of removing a swallowed hook from bleeding gills.

It's a complex set of issues for young kids to process, and I am thankful for these moments with my sons, and for these fish. I did this with my father and brother, and watching my boys catch these fish feels like continuity.

Rachel Pollack writes that the Sun in the tarot tradition points to happiness, contentment, bringing people together. There is a physicality to the card, a childlike joy.

In these moments with the bluegill flapping on the dock, my sons screaming with laughter, I feel that radiant energy.

Many of the traditional tarot representations of the sun feature children, innocent and protected. It reminds me of being a kid, the bluegill protecting the offspring, my relationship with my young boys.

Our sun is the source of all energy. Like a good father, it holds the world safely in its orbit. Its seeming constancy renews our faith in an ordered cosmos.

The sun is a middle-aged, unremarkable ball of gas – one of 100 billion others in the Milky Way galaxy. But it is our everything—the source of our food, the weather, the energy that drives our planet.

It feels like a saccharine cliché, but nothing is more reassuring that everything will be OK than sitting in the warm sun with my kids and some worms catching bluegill.

JUDGEMENT

CHAPTER 20
ANSWERING THE CALL

The cicadas have been winding down. Chitinous, black bodies crunch underfoot on my driveway every time I step out the front door.

The last of the cicadas in my neighborhood stutter and whir, looking for a mate in the waning swarm. It's last call. The party is nearly over. All but the next generation are either dead or dying.

Flagging brown leaves give a sense that the fall is arriving early. Female cicadas have deposited eggs in the tips of deciduous tree branches, and many of clusters of leaves have turned brown, branch tips drooping. The twigs will drop and the rice-sized larvae will burrow into the ground and begin another long cycle.

In late May 2016, hordes of large insects emerged from the ground in patches of woods all over eastern Ohio.

"It was epic," says naturalist and music professor Lisa Rainsong, who witnessed an emergence at Geauga Park District's Big Creek. "I'd never seen this before, the whole ground was moving as the cicadas were climbing out of their holes and up our legs. When they split their nymphal skins, the white cicadas dangled like Christmas ornaments. When they inflated their new wings they just looked like angels.

"Many of the insects didn't make it, emerging with deformed wings. Everything was happening right there, and it was emotionally overwhelming. I came home and couldn't talk, didn't turn on the computer. I needed to process this."

The brown nymphal insects crawl out of holes in the dirt,

and then climb onto any vertical surface to molt into the adult form. The back of the exoskeleton splits open and the white adult form emerges, pulsing and writhing. The cicadas lean back, and loosen themselves from their exoskeletons, crawl from their husks, and pump their wings with fluid. You would find the exoskeletons still clinging to tree trunks everywhere.

The cicadas spent seventeen years alone underground, clinging to tree roots before joining their cohorts in the trees for a summer of flying and mating.

The symbolism echoes the tarot card Judgement—the card typically depicts a winged angel awakening the dead. It signifies a change—the end of one phase and the beginning of another. The call from the angel is a summons.

"It can seem as if something within the person has already decided and the only choice left to the conscious self is to follow the appropriate action," writes Rachel Pollack in *Seventy-Eight Degrees of Wisdom*. "A force greater than yourself is calling you. The title of the card implies to judge, or to be judged – but the meaning doesn't suggest you must change, but that you already have. We don't really know ourselves, and cannot, until we hear and respond to the call."

In the Cuyahoga Valley National Park in the last week of May, I started spotting them in the low saplings. A dozen black and orange adult cicadas and empty, translucent nymphal husks clung to each small tree. The newly emerged insects barely moved.

Each passing day, more cicadas emerged. One morning, my three young boys hiked through a meadow on the Buckeye Trail, and found so many slow-moving insects, we could comb a half-dozen cicadas into each hand with a single swipe of the tall prairie weeds. They wouldn't bite or sting, but just clung to our fingers and shirts.

We placed them on our heads, let them cling to our backs. We let them crawl all over us.

Periodical cicadas are found only in eastern North America. There are seven species—four with thirteen-year life cycles and three with seventeen-year cycles. Of these, there are about fifteen distinct broods—geographic areas where the periodical cicadas emerge en masse in predictable time tables.

Brood V is a medium-sized emergence, and stretches from eastern Ohio to Western PA and northern West Virginia, with oddball pockets in Virginia and Long Island, NY. It features all three species of 17-year cicada. All of the seventeen-year species basically look alike—big black insects with orange accents and red eyes. But each species differs in song.

Rainsong helped me better understand what I was hearing in the middle of the emergence.

We met at the Bath Nature Preserve, we could hear *Magicicada septendecim* all around us. A high-pitched, eerie warble.

The chorus of cicadas sounded like a single note, and Rainsong sang it matching the pitch. "It's probably about an E," she said, taking out her digital tuner app on the cell phone to confirm.

"It sounds like a single pitch, but each cicada singing 'pharaoh, pharaoh.' There's a drop at the end," Rainsong said. "When it drops it's the end of the song, and the pitch falls. But when there's a whole wall of cicadas singing, we don't hear the drop offs. It's a complex sound."

She and I walked the bridle trail on this rolling, 410-acre property west of Akron. The landscape is a mix of meadows, restored wetlands, and beech-maple forests. The property was once owned by the Firestone family, and now serves as a wildlife refuge, and research station for the University of Akron biology programs.

Later that day, I heard the cicada that sounded more like what I expected—like a person running a weedwhacker over an uneven, scrubby hillside. It was an oscillating ticking, mechanical and rhythmic noise. Like someone playing a bullroarer. These were

Magicicada cassini.

We did not immediately hear any *Magicicada septendecula*, which have a more rhythmic version of the *M. cassini* call.

As we walked the bridle trail we came to a bowl, a natural amphitheater where the sound of two species of cicadas grew and swelled in waves. This was the place where Rainsong would bring author and musician David Rothenberg later that week to perform with the singing insects.

Teneral insects crawled in the tall grass, remarkably agreeable and docile bugs. Hundreds or even thousands of cicadas flew between the tree tops overhead as we listened to the drone—the song swelling into a crescendo.

"It seems like the pitch of the song has gotten higher as the day warmed up," Rainsong said, looking again at the tuner. "Yep, it's gone up almost a half step. There is something so cool about learning something new. Hopefully I'll be out in the field for the next emergence, as I'll be seventy-nine."

A few days later, I joined an audience of about thirty people to listen to one of the strangest musical performances of my life. David Rothenberg and Czech composer Lucie Vítková led our group through the Bath Nature Preserve, and stopped beside a path where the cicadas were singing and flying.

Rothenberg had authored the book *Bug Music: How Insects Gave Us Rhythm and Noise* in 2013, and had been staging interspecies performances around the country, coordinating musically with singing insects emergences in various broods.

"Life is a vast music with irregular rhythms swirling op top of one another, which we can choose to tap into and appraise when we wish," wrote Rothenberg.

Cicadas flew overhead as clouds scudded past quickly on the wind. Vítková and Rothenberg brought out a portable, cylindrical speaker and began making tentative sounds on their instruments—Rothenberg on clarinet, and Vítková playing electronic music on an iPad.

I watched Rothenberg twitch and sway. Vítková picked up a harmonica, and then played an ancient Japanese double-reed instrument.

"One of the ways to learn about something is to join in," Rothenberg said.

"Art and science come together in unusual ways. I can make one performance with humans and music, and it can be beautiful and successful. But for science, I'd need to do it 1,000 times—to analyze it in a statistical manner. It's a different criteria for truth. I want to develop a piece of music that learns from the animal world."

To perceive these insect sounds as music changes our relationship with nature. These rhythms and sounds are much more accessible to us if we consider them aesthetically, rather than focusing on a communicated message.

In *Bug Music*, Rothenberg suggests that the individual noises, the high frequency vibrations of tymbals or drumlike organs on the cicadas, are part of a vast rhythm. The whole emergence can be seen as a single beat, set to swell and repeat as a macrosound, coalescing at this prime-numbered seventeen-year pattern.

Seventeen years feels like a strangely satisfying period to divide up phases of a life.

This was my third emergence of the Brood V Periodical cicada. The first emergence happened when I was four, but I must have been too young to retain a memory. The second happened when I was twenty-one—and I was almost certainly too drunk and foolish to have been paying any attention.

Now thirty-eight, I watched this emergence closely. The next two are somewhat ominous—fifty-five and seventy-two. It somehow makes those future versions of myself more real. Twenty-one doesn't feel like it was that long ago.

Fifty-five will be here sooner than I hope.

There's something about this seventeen-year rhythm of a cicada emergence that inspires us to reflect. It reminds us that we haven't always been attentive. It connects us to the landscape and the past.

I think about why the seventeen-year cycle developed, how the various broods formed. I think about the changes in the landscape, the loss of chestnut trees, and now the loss of ash. They've survived tens of thousands of years, and will persist.

I wonder if all of the people I care about will be here for the next beat, the next cycle. I worry about how much of this I will remember next time. Will I remember the way the bugs swarmed in the treetops outside my bedroom window, how they climbed over my boys?

The next time they come, all of my babies that I could carry in my arms will be grown men.

The woods are too quiet now.

XXI

THE WORLD

CHAPTER 21
THE ABUNDANCE, DIVERSITY AND LOSS

Is it not a maimed and imperfect nature that I am conversant with?
—Henry David Thoreau

The Lake Erie landscape is explosively fertile.

From September till ice-up, millions of walleye will migrate and feed, moving from the eastern corner of the lake to the shallow western basin. Clevelanders will flock to the city breakwalls at night to catch them.

Ring-billed gulls, Bonaparte's gulls, herring gulls wheel overhead and out over the water, chasing emerald shiners. Hundreds of thousands of gulls stop over in the Great Lakes each winter on migrations from the Canadian Arctic to the Gulf or Atlantic Coasts. Over a dozen species of gulls can visit Northeast Ohio in the winter.

In October, huge numbers of loons, grebes, and diving ducks funnel out of Alaska and Canada to spend a few weeks on the south shore of our lake.

Up to a quarter million red-breasted mergansers may stop refuel on Lake Erie's abundant baitfish each winter. Flocks of tens of thousands are common, floating right off the shoreway.

Predators converge from above and below to eat the silvery shoals of small fish. Everywhere, there is life.

This shoreline is still one of richest ecosystems in the United States and is a critical stopover on our hemisphere's most spectacular bird migrations.

USA Today listed Lake Erie's Magee Marsh as the nation's top birdwatching destination in 2014.

Nearly every species of songbird in Ohio visits this tiny patch of wet woods each spring, but the crowds are here for the warblers, colorful migratory insectivores.

Nearly forty species of warbler frequent Magee Marsh.

Most warblers overwinter in Mexico, Central America, and the Caribbean, over 2,500 miles away. On their way back north to their breeding grounds in Canada each spring, a world-famous diversity and density of warblers spends a few days refueling in this patch of woods just outside Toledo.

While this diversity and abundance is incredible, it is hard to convey the grandiosity of the wildlife of Lake Erie prior to European settlement.

The Great Lakes once boasted giant predatory lake trout that could grow to a wolf-sized seventy pounds and eight-foot-long lake sturgeon. The lake trout are gone, and the sturgeon are dwindling.

In 1799, Irish explorer Isaac Weld wrote in his book *Travels* that so many animals were being carried down Niagara Falls where Lake Erie flows into the Niagara River and Lake Ontario, that "a dreadful stench arises from the quantity of putrid matter lying on the shore, and numberless birds of prey, attracted by it, are always seen hovering about the place."

Researchers estimated at that time more than a hundred fish passed over Niagara Falls each second. Nothing like that superabundance is evident today.

"The native wildlife of the Great Lakes country is a shadow of its former self," writes John Riley in *The Once and Future Great Lakes Country*. "Where wildlife was once abundant and muscular on the land, the faint modern irruptions of boreal passerines heading south when their crop trees fail, or of owls in the winter, go largely unnoticed. Today, even a hint of abundance, like deer in Pennsylvania, or raccoons in Toronto, or Canada geese, or opossum moving north, makes us nervous. The first instinct is that these are possible vectors of disease, rather than likely indicators of health and plenty."

Billions of passenger pigeons once darkened the skies of the Great Lakes for nights and days on end. The sheer weight of these birds broke down trees in their roosting areas. Feces piled up to a foot deep at their roosts, fertilizing the ground.

"It is believed that this species once constituted 25 to 40 percent of the total bird population of the United States," writes the Smithsonian's curator of vertebrate zoology. "One of the last authenticated records of the capture of a wild bird was at in Pike County, Ohio, on 24 March 1900."

The birds relied on huge tracts of forest in the Great Lakes for roosting sites and food.

Around 80 percent of the Great Lakes land was forested in 1600 when pre-Columbian cultural practices and agricultural traditions were intact.

Following the collapse of native people, the percentage of forested land spiked above 90 percent. Then European settlers in our region cleared the primeval woods so that 6 percent of original forest remained by 1920.

American chestnuts once made up 25 percent of the deciduous forest in the eastern United States, but the chestnut blight, first discovered in New York in 1904, completely destroyed the entire forest population. We will never see the giant chestnut trees our great-grandparents grew up with.

And we are losing more tree species diversity rapidly due to beech bark disease, emerald ash borers, Dutch elm disease, butternut canker, hemlock woolly adelgid, oak wilt, and Asian longhorned beetle.

We've also lost the major megafauna.

On Christmas Eve in 1818, some 600 hunters slaughtered 21 bears, 17 wolves, 300 deer, and hundreds of smaller animals that were thought to be threatening the farm crops and livestock during the Great Hinckley Hunt, twenty-five miles south of Cleveland.

According to an account by Charles Neil in *History of Medina County and Ohio*: "The order was that the farmers gather by early daybreak, armed with rifles, guns, pitchforks, flails, clubs, and every available implement of war; form a continuous line on the four sides of the township, and, at a given signal, advance toward its center, killing, shooting and slaughtering all game that came within reach."

With so many populations of animals gutted, the land itself has drifted away from a mix of mature forests, prairies, and swamps, to a denuded and diminished landscape without many key players. The plants and animals lived in a codependent state of flux and renewal.

"What happens when you remove most (and in some cases all) of the dominant fauna from the richest temperate freshwater landscape in the world over two centuries? And then simultaneously reduce to life-support levels the numbers of most other native vertebrates? What happens when you remove so many species in such numbers? The result is what we have around today," writes Riley.

Edward O. Wilson writes in *The Creation*, "With the global species extinction rate now exceeding the global species birthrate at least a hundredfold, and soon to increase ten times that much, and with the birth rate falling through the loss of sites where evolution can occur; the number of species is plummeting. The original level of biodiversity is not likely to be regained in any period of time that has meaning for the human mind."

Wilson describes the coming age as the Eremozoic Era— The Age of Loneliness.

I don't list these losses to leave you with a sense of despair. The landscape once supported gatherings of wildlife in biblical proportions and could again.

The meaning of the World card in tarot is abundance, achievement, and reward.

I want to leave you with the impression that our home has a potential to be one of the wildest, most fecund places on the planet.

Where the Great Plains meet the Alleghenies and the boreal forest meets the temperate deciduous, we find a lot of species diversity. Ohio is a population boundary or habitat edge for a lot of species.

These animals living on the boundaries of their habitat range are more likely to develop the biological diversity to ensure overall species resiliency. The genetics of the animals thriving in our southernmost, shallowest Great Lake might be incredibly important to the overall health of species in the future.

We still have two-foot-long amphibians, eastern hellbenders, lurking in our rivers. Ancient-looking spotted gar swim in our Great Lake. Massasauga rattlesnakes hunt voles in the wet meadows east of Cleveland, and native brook trout are swimming in a few streams.

I tell you these things to repeat the names, so that you will know they are there. I write about these lives so that we can make contact with the world beyond our material culture, to inspire wonder.

Cohabitating a world with an abundance and diversity of animals has always been a part of basic human experience. In fact, equating animals with happiness has been hardwired into our psyche. Look at children's cartoons and toys, made up almost entirely of anthropomorphic representations of animals, telling our kids that they're not alone in this world.

Even as habitat loss wipes out individual animals, species, and even entire earth processes, we will still be surrounded by some forms of resilient, wildlife.

Nature dies hard. It may not be as diverse or beautiful as

what existed just a couple generations before, but it is still there.

There is still plenty of time to roll in the dirt in the forest. Stare out at Lake Erie. Listen to the wind. Don't live separately from the world. Don't despair.

ACKNOWLEDGEMENTS

I'd like to dedicate this book to my wife and children, and to my parents, who brought my brother and me into the woods.

This work wouldn't be possible without the support of Northeast Ohio's naturalist and biology community. I want to give special thanks to Lisa Rainsong, Jen Brumfield, Mike Durkalec, Ben Piazza, Jamey Emmert, Jim McCormac, Andy Jones, and a whole host of other folks who have been incredibly generous with their time and knowledge. And also, thanks to Anne Trubek and Belt for believing in this crazy project.

Special thanks to Martha Bayne for excellent editing, and Rachel Pollack, Lisa Courturier, Kenn Kaufman, and David George Haskell for their inspiration and support.

ABOUT THE AUTHOR

Matt Stansberry was born in Akron, Ohio and graduated from Kent State University. He writes about the intersection of natural history and myth. Matt spent six years in Oregon writing about wild trout and salmon and advocating for sustainable fisheries management. He currently lives in North Carolina with his wife and three sons.

ABOUT THE ILLUSTRATOR

David Wilson is an illustrator from Brimfield, Ohio who has worked for *The Atlantic, New York Magazine,* the *Boston Globe,* and many other outlets. He also produces independent comics and films. He currently lives in Ohio with his wife and two daughters. More of his work can be found at www.workdavidwork.com.